SURREAL

OR

SO REAL

Which do you prefer?

Barbara van den Akker
May 2012

1

✝

"That I may know Him and the power of His
resurrection and the fellowship of His sufferings
being made conformable unto His death; if by
any means I might attain unto the resurrection
of the dead. Not as though I had already attained
either were already perfect: but I follow after, if that I
may apprehend that for which also I am apprehended
of Christ Jesus. Brethren, I count not myself to have
apprehended: but this one thing I do, forgetting those
things which are behind and reaching forth unto
those things which are before I press toward the mark
for the prize of the high calling of God in Christ Jesus."

Phil. 3:10-14 (KJV)

©ISBN-13:978-1480237605

3

†

This book is dedicated to my husband, Wim, now with the Lord in Glory and whom God used to teach me, among other things, the difference between religion and relationship.

†

ONE

Before I was born again of God's Holy Spirit I believed in God. That belief had no power when life got tough, nor did the religion to which I had been so faithful.

Scripture says the devils believe and tremble but it does them no good. Nor does it for any human being.

It was not until the Father revealed Jesus to me that power came into my life.

Power to forgive.

Power to stay in an unfortunate circumstance.

Power to praise God in the face of heartbreak.

Power to thank God in and for all situations that He allowed and even occasioned in my life.

Power – real, true power!

Up to that time I had gone to church faithfully and often. I gave when and where I was supposed to give. I obeyed all the ordinances. I was a good girl. I prayed. I was in the choir. But there was no power for living the life I had to live. There was no power and there were no answers.

I was about to walk away from religion, all the while blaming God.

But God Who is rich in mercy, God Who answers prayer (my sisters and others were praying), looked down on a day early in January 1974 and revealed Jesus to me and:

  opened my spiritual eyes
   opened my spiritual ears
    took my heart of stone and replaced it with a
     heart of flesh and
      put a new spirit within me (Himself)

all in less than an instant

     He saved me
      chose me
       called me
        forgave me
         reconciled me
          justified me
           sanctified me
            cleansed me
             glorified me
              sealed me
               adopted me

Now that is REAL !

No more wondering if maybe UFO's were for real.
No more thinking maybe we did come from slime.
No more thinking, "Is this all there is?" NO!
REAL changed all of that forever. I had gone from believing (and wondering) to knowing. God took

Himself out of my Believer and put Himself into
my Knower. - Yup! That's REAL ! And it had
nothing to do with religion...

†

TWO

I started thinking about all of this when I told the pastor of the church I was then attending what had happened to me. That he had no clue was more than obvious. Shock overwhelmed me.

I thought I was the only one who had not "gotten" it. I was wrong. This was a whole new ball game.

That was in 1974 and I didn't know the word surreal existed. Now I know I was religiously living in the surreal. I also know that I was not the only one.

Many people grow up in religion and by rote they continue on in whatever the belief system they have been taught. While it is true that some do seek and find the Living God while in their religious system, very few think and reach beyond the roof of religion. When I consider that fact I am amazed that any of us really do get saved.

For that reason, I am blessed that God gave us the gift of prayer and the blessing of missionaries. I am grateful that He put it on His people's hearts to spread the Good News of salvation through the Lord Jesus Christ.

But man is not saved because he reaches up to God through religion. Man is saved because God, through Jesus, reached down to man. Praise Him! How humbling is that for the Living Almighty God!

†

THREE

In 1974 my marriage was falling apart. I had three preschool babies. I had my lawyer picked out and my emotions vacillated between numb and silent screaming.

To add to the confusion and conflict my sisters were studying the Bible with a minister of another denomination. Sigh….. They kept using words like born again and salvation. I really wanted off this planet. It was all just too much.

Then one day my sister, Geri, called me. We had a long telephone conversation during which she told me she knew she was going to Heaven. I told her she was living in the sin of presumption and it went from there. She remained calm and kept giving me Biblical illustrations, like the thief on the cross. I was not calm and ended up hanging up on her.

Two days later she called again. I was upstairs making beds and very frustrated that she had the nerve to push this 'stuff' again.

But she said there was a man on the radio right then and he could explain it all better than she could so why didn't I put it on and listen. To shut her up, I did. That's when REAL began.

After assuring Geri I would listen and with the sheet from the as yet unmade bed still on my arm I placed the phone in its cradle and proceeded toward the boys' room to finish Bill's bed.

I got as far as the hallway. There was a fog I could not see but could *feel*. The radio was on but I could not make sense of the words spoken. It was as if he was speaking a foreign language.

I thought I was having a stroke or something and I thought, "I'm not going to let this get the best of me. I'm just going to keep going."

I got to the boys' bedroom and went to throw the sheet onto Bill's bed when the room was suddenly filled with light. Bright light. Brighter than day. I turned to see who had turned it on.

When I turned, my head became a funnel. All the light in the room rushed into the funnel and filled my being. With it came five points of knowledge.

Jesus was that Light.
    Jesus was God.
        Jesus died on the cross for *my* sins.
            I was going to be with Him forever.
                Everything I'd heard about Him my whole life was true.

Yup! Surreal was now SO REAL !

The weight of the world was lifted off my shoulders and that sheet and I did a hallelujah dance in that bedroom and life has never been the same.

Now I don't expect everyone to have such an experience. I was so steeped in religion and my own problems that it took a sledge hammer to get my attention. But some kind of an experience is necessary with the Living God. Jesus promised that He and His Father and His Holy Spirit would come and live in, make Their home in, His disciples. Jesus told them to WAIT for it to happen. We have to do the same. Ask for it. Wait for it.

While waiting, read the Word (the Bible) and pray. Believe me, when the One Who created all there is, seen and unseen, comes and indwells your being you cannot help but know it. He is worth the wait. You will have the Creator living within you and you will have the birthmarks of the born again.

It really hurts my heart when I am in church – any church – and conversation turns to Jesus and I mention something that He did in my life recently and conversation stops and then changes.

It is a dead give away. One of the symptoms of surreal religion is an unhealthy fear of having a relationship with the Living God. Fear of a God Who actually talks with you and shows Himself REAL. Religion is safe. Jesus is risk. In reality the opposite is true.

The reason for that is because the spirit realm is real. Forever is real. When one settles for religion one risks their entire future. Jesus, Himself, said unless one is born again he cannot enter the Kingdom of Heaven. Only in Jesus is our forever secure. So in reality, Jesus is safe and religion is risk.

Do not misunderstand. I am not against religion. We all need religion and we need it for many reasons. But if all we have is religion, even with all the right words, in reality we have nothing. We are living in a dream – surreal.

We can join the choir, teach Sunday school, be a deacon, be on the missions board, be on the church board, we can even be a pastor, unless we have Jesus, the risen, living Person, indwelling us we have nothing. Simple as that.

Intellectual or even emotional assent is not enough. Religious agreement is not enough. Peer pressure pleasing is not enough. Nothing is enough save Jesus Christ Himself.

And He is there. He is waiting with open arms for any and all who will come to Him. That, after all, is what this whole rigmarole is all about – Jesus giving Himself for man, all men of all times in all places. "For God so loved the world that He gave His only begotten Son that whosoever believes in Him should not perish but have eternal life. For God sent not His Son into the world to condemn the world; but that the world through Him might be saved." Simple as that. Amazing as that.

†

FOUR

What is even sadder, I think, than the fact that there
are multitudes of people in churches who believe
they are safe when indeed they are not, is the fact
that there are multitudes of Christians, truly born
again people, who are afraid to be too close to the
risen Lord. Afraid of the supernatural. Sigh....

The first words God speaks to His people all
throughout the scriptures are, "Fear not." Yes, we
are to have a healthy fear of the Lord, but not when
we are born again and in His presence. Then we are
to allow His love for us as His children to overcome
that fear (out balance it) and – fear not. Yet we
fear. Perhaps it is mostly fear of the unknown. It is
almost as if it is OK for God to speak to us through
His Word, but not in Person, not up close and real.

How sad. All God longs for is close, personal
relationship with us. In Jeremiah He tells us that it
is not our sacrifices (religious rites) He wants but
He wants us to know Him.

In John, Jesus proclaims that eternal life is to know
God and the One He sent. Not to know about Him,
but to know Him. How do you know someone if
you do not spend time with them? Jesus rose from
the dead. He is alive. He said, "My sheep hear My
voice." He wants us to have conversation with
Him. He wants us to know Him and to know that
we know that we know that He knows us. It is the
deepest and most precious relationship we will ever
or could ever have.

†

FIVE

I realize there is a risk when we enter the spirit realm. Risk that we do not hear the Holy Spirit but some foul demon posing as an angel of light. That is remedied by knowing the Word of God and our wanting God's will for our lives rather than our own will for our lives. When those two requirements are met, God will protect us. If we cannot trust Him for that how can we trust Him to get us to Heaven? How big is our God anyway?

Yes, those requirements demand work and humility. Work to read and know and study the Word and to filter all we hear through it. Humility to lay down our own hopes and dreams and ambitions and expectations and replace them with whatever God in His infinite wisdom and love ordained for our lives from before He laid the foundation of the world. Ephesians 2:10 is very clear about that fact.

In our self-centered culture that is antithesis to all we hear and read, but it is an unmovable fact for a Christian. God does not change with the whims of culture. We must say as did Jesus, "Nevertheless, not My will but Thine be done."

I'm almost 72 and have arthritis and agree with those who say growing old is not for sissies. I have news for you, neither is Christianity! It is impossible without faith and faith is hard work.

Without faith it is impossible to please God. What is faith? Something you conjure up? NO. The

Word is very clear about that. Faith is a gift of God. Whether it comes in the form of a measure (which every man is given) or a gift of the Holy Spirit or the fruit of the Holy Spirit, it is from God; and therefore we must spend time with God to receive it.

Hebrews tells us faith is a substance. It is obviously not a natural tangible substance. Therefore it is a spiritual substance. When we spend time with God in Spirit and in Truth, time in His presence in sweet relationship with Him, we receive faith. We can't feel it. We can't see it. But when we are in life's circumstances it is that faith that empowers us to act and react in ways that are pleasing to God and according to His Word rather than our own human nature.

It is that faith which empowered all the heroes of the faith listed in Hebrews 11 to go through all they went through. It is that faith which empowered all those in Foxe's Book of Martyrs (Please do read it if you have not.) to go through what they went through. It is that faith which empowers brothers and sisters in Christ all over the world today to endure patiently the race set before them. Without faith it is impossible! And that is why Satan and his cohorts will do all they can to keep us from a deeper relationship with God. They do not want us to receive that faith! They will tell us it is not necessary for everyone or that we are too tired to read the Word, we don't have to study the Word, we don't have time to pray and besides others are praying, etc., etc. ad nauseam. Most of all, those demons will try their best to keep us afraid of the supernatural world. But "…greater is He Who is in you than he who is in the world." has never changed! We need to push on till we have that overcoming victory.

On top of that many Christians today act as did Job before he knew God. Job 13:15 is perhaps the most misquoted verse in the Bible. Job does say, "Though He slay me, yet will I trust in Him," but he continues that same sentence by saying, *"but I will maintain my own ways before Him."* What incongruity! You can't trust God and have your own way at the same time. It just does not work that way! This was said when Job was a believer but not yet a knower. However it works the same way for both the born again and the not yet born again.

Take a minute and go to the end of Job…chapter 42, verses 5 and 6. Here we see the result of a person being brought by God from surreal religion into real relationship. Job says, "I have heard of Thee by the hearing of the ear; but now mine eye seeth Thee and I abhor myself and repent in dust and ashes."

In other words, I went to church and heard of You all my life and believed it all; but now You have revealed Yourself to me and I have gone from believing to knowing.

It is then that we see ourselves as the sinners that we are because it is then that we see God's pure holiness. How can we do other than repent?

When my sister, Geri, witnessed to me that day in 1974 it was because she knew her Spirit did not witness to the spirit that was within me. Before I was born again I had visions, I heard God talk to me, I was very religious. But God did not live inside of me. Therein is the difference. She pushed on and I am forever grateful that she did. I would not have seen the Light had I not been in darkness.

Because I had these religious experiences I had one sister convinced I was as 'Christian' as was she. But Geri knew better. She knew that portion of the Word that says that the Spirit bears witness to our spirit. Religious experiences do not cause us to be born again! Indeed they can be ploys of the enemy to keep us from the real thing; as well they can be God calling us to Himself and we for whatever reason do not go beyond the experience to the Living God.

Perhaps you know someone in the same boat. Please do not settle for where they are or are not. Please have the courage and love to go after them in whatever way God's Holy Spirit might lead you. They may not need a sledge hammer as did I but everyone needs at least a hammer and chisel. Chipping away a little bit at a time. All of forever is at stake. Hell is as real as Heaven and all of us are going to live forever in one place or the other. They are both very REAL.

†

SIX

Another surreal idea people have is that after they come to Jesus life will be a bed of roses. There are preachers today telling people God wants them to be happy and prosperous, to live like king's kids. Those preachers are making a great deal of money on this earth but will have much to answer for when they meet God. Remember, Moses could not enter the Promised Land because he misrepresented God to the people. These preachers are doing the same thing. Dangerous place to be.

We are King's kids; but our Father's Kingdom is not of this world. Not for us as it was not for Jesus. The happiness they preach is a matter of life's circumstance. The joy and peace Jesus gives is constant and far surpasses what the world calls 'happy'. It does not vary with our life's conditions. Prosperity from Jesus' point of view has almost nothing to do with finances. It has to do with the condition of our hearts and minds and relationships. God's economy is not at all what man's economy equates to be.

Rather, this earth is a kind of school, a learning place, for Christians. It is here we learn God's precepts and His ways. The criteria I've mentioned before: We must read, study and know the Word and we must want His will in our lives and give up our own. Simple. Not easy, but simple. We need to stop listening to teachings that contradict what we know is right. Right is what is according to God's Word. Period.

I am more and more convinced that much of the New Testament was written to Christians living in the SURREAL rather than the SO REAL. When we read the Word we need to see with eyes that do not filter through the spectacles of other men's teachings. The Holy Spirit is our Teacher.

It is as if we have two buildings within our breast. One is a Temple of Truth. The other is a warehouse of information. Everything – even the Word – we read or hear must go into the warehouse of information. Only the Holy Spirit has the right to take bricks of Truth from it and place them onto our Temple of Truth. You see, there are more ways than one that we are the Temple of the Holy Spirit.... The fact that He lives in us makes us His Temple. That will never change. But the knowledge we have of the spiritual realm, the knowledge we have of Who He is and the knowledge we have of what He expects in relationship with us is built by Him alone! The first is a gift from Him. It indeed is our very salvation. The second involves our heart and mind. It is how we translate the spiritual into the natural and are able to give an answer to every man who asks of the hope that is within us. They are both gifts from God but we have a very definite part to play. We must learn the Word and stay in close personal relationship, even breath by breath, with the Lord Jesus Christ, with His (and our) Father and with the Holy Spirit. Only this will keep us in reality. Only this will give us all we need to walk in victory over our flesh, the world and the devil.

†

SEVEN

The older I get and the more I know and learn of God the shorter my prayers become. Why? Because I see how mighty and far above mankind He is. I see how foolish it is for us to even think we can direct the One Who spoke and the heaven and the earth simply was, Who spoke and the universe with all its solar systems fell into place, Who created all that is seen and unseen…how we can direct Him to 'fix' things. Talk about surreal!

He sees what we do not see. He knows what we do not know. He plans what we cannot even think of or imagine.

Recently I've seen on DVD's teachings by men who have investigated astronomy and the human body, teaching me all over again how small we are and how much bigger God is than anything we can imagine. My thinking and now my prayers are often more groans and feelings than words.

Yet He tells us to come with words to Him in prayer. Oh, Dear Reader, let us let those words be REAL and not religious or self-righteous mumbo jumbo. Better to wait on the Holy Spirit to give us the words to pray than to bring meaningless and/or presumptuous chatter to Him.

Often He leads us to pray back the Word to Him. Not in a 'demanding' way but in a way which agrees with Him, what He proclaims to be important. For example, that we might walk worthy of the calling to all pleasing or that we might seek first His Kingdom and His righteousness, etc. That works, that's real. It took me years to learn this truth about REAL prayer.

†

EIGHT

You may wonder what happened back there in 1974 after the Father called me to Jesus and revealed Him to me and the Triune God came and indwelt me, invaded my life really. My entire being changed. All my hopes and dreams and expectations and ambitions and goals changed. I won't go into the whole story, but within three months my husband had an even more dramatic experience with the Living God. Life changed.

But it was not all roses and cream. It was hard work. As time went on it became even harder. Perhaps some day that story will be told but for now suffice it to say that I learned the hard way that we do not come with our laundry/shopping list to God when we pray. We come humbly before His Throne and wait on Him. We come with thanksgiving and praise because He is worthy of such. We present our problems and leave them in His capable hands. He has a plan. That is enough. Whether His answer is to our liking or is negative to our wishes it comes to be okay. Paul said that in whatsoever state he was in he had learned to be content. We stay with God in prayer until His peace reigns once again in our heart and we wonder how we ever even survived in surreal…. No matter how He answers our prayer.

†

NINE

Perhaps this is a good place to share others' stories. To share lives that were also taken from SURREAL to SO REAL. They are shared that you might be encouraged to come to the Living God in Spirit and in Truth and allow Him His way in your life. I know each of the men and women sharing their lives here and can attest to their veracity. With only minor grammatical editing they are just as written by each of them.

As you will see, their stories are as varied as are the people themselves. They come from several different backgrounds and denominations. But God works in each one as He wills. Each one is different, unique. God shows no partiality nor does He esteem any religion or social standing above another. He desires that all come to Him and to that end He is working in all mankind.

TESTIMONIES

†

When I was young I was taught at church about God but not how to know Him as I do now.

My life was one of emotional pain and looking for love in all the wrong places due to circumstances that don't need telling. I did things my way without thought of consequences. I became filled with guilt and shame and fear.

After three children and a divorce I had an experience with God. I felt His love for me and His arms wrapped around me enveloping me in that love. But I was not ready to turn my life over to Him so I continued in a life of sin and rebellion for another five years.

Then I went to a religious group, to a prayer meeting, to a women's Bible study and to a Billy Graham crusade where I said the words to be born again. I did not realize it but this was only the beginning of my journey and I thought I would never sin again.

However, God allowed me to fall into sin and I was devastated. So I agreed to go to a tent meeting in Bermuda where I finally surrendered all to God and received the Holy Spirit. I was in His presence for at least an hour, pinned to the ground. My hands and feet were as if they were nailed to the ground. No one touched me or prayed over me. It was me and God and that was when I finally received the power to persevere with God. That was when I had the power to stop giving in to my own real or imagined needs.

Now, many years later, as I walk my daily walk, with all the many temptations, the Holy Spirit convicts me of any sin and convinces me of righteousness because He is real! It is not simply a religious rite or peer pressure. I always have the choice to hear and obey or hear and rebel. But even when I fall, and I do fall, I have the power to confess my sin and continue on with the Lord.

I have learned to know God and His ways and His plan for my life. It is not always easy but it is always better when I stay in right relationship with Him and through Him with others.

Maureen Doyle
East Bridgewater, MA

†

This one from a gal we will call Jane. She is a dear friend but prefers her name not be used.

I grew up in a small one-blinking light town in northern New England. My family and I faithfully attended a local church. I was a choir member and a perfect-attendance child at Sunday school. Church was the culturally and socially correct thing for us.

I married my high school sweetheart and after other moves ended up in Massachusetts.

When my next door neighbor was witnessing to me I dismissed her as a Jesus freak until my husband left me.   Then I joined her at church.

On Palm Sunday I accepted the Lord and for the first time I had excitement and joy and peace all mingled together with the pain of my husband's leaving.

Surrounded by Christians, God has filled my life with Himself and His people. He was real. Now almost 30 years later, He still is.

†

If you asked me as I was growing up if I was a
Christian I would have said, "Yes", I was. I went to
church every week (one of the main denominations)
and I sang in the choir. I tried to be a good person.
I believed in God Who was three in one. I went to
Sunday school and learned about Jesus. Yes, I was
a Christian.

As I grew up and had children I dedicated them to
God in the church and in my prayers. I made
mistakes, yes, but I was a Christian, a good person.

Or so I thought......

In my mid twenties I began to realize something
was missing in my life spiritually (although I didn't
realize the spiritual part) I started reading books
which led me into studying reincarnation, Edgar
Casey, etc. This was in the 1970's. I still went to
church every Sunday and was involved in various
groups – even vacation Bible school and Sunday
school.

I thought of myself as a good person. We even took
in foster babies at that time. Yes, I was a Christian.

Unknown to me at this time, a 19-year old neighbor,
a Baptist, started to pray for me. She talked to me
and told me about Christian radio. I started
listening and soon was listening every day. I began
to read my Bible more. As a preacher would say
the sinner's prayer I would repeat it, over and
over...

One March day in 1976 as I was hanging out diapers in my back yard, suddenly the sky became bluer and more beautiful. I stopped hanging diapers and looked up. I felt suddenly as if I had lived my entire life up until this moment in a shoe box with the lid closed. Suddenly the lid opened and I saw that there was so much more available. I had come out of the darkness into the Light. I told the Lord that I gave Him my life and the lives of my family at that moment. I didn't know the words for this experience but I had been born again.

Later I was led to a Charismatic meeting and began to attend regularly. Soon I was baptized in the Spirit. Life has never been the same. Now if you ask me if I am a Christian you will get an enthusiastic YES!

I had much to learn about this new life I was living. My friends and I devoured the Bible. We had so much to learn. Over the past 36 years I have learned to walk with the Lord in areas of joy and pain and sorrow. He has never left me or forsaken me and always, in each situation, has given me the ability to go through, whether joy or pain, learning more and more about Him Who is the author and finisher of my faith.

As a child and young adult I lived by every emotion I felt. As a believer I have learned not to live by my emotions or even to trust them, for I know that God's Word has the answer for each situation in my life. As I learn more and more about HIM, I concentrate less and less on me.

I teach a small Bible study and am active in my church. I am walking in the blessings of God each and every day. I am living in the Light and have never gone back to the darkness. People who know me say there is something different about me: a peace and a strength that they can see. It is the presence of God in my life shining through. Wherever I go I want people to see the life of Jesus working in me. I want them to know that I am a Christian.

Marsha Barry
(whose name is written in the Lamb's Book of Life)

†

My amazing journey from religion to relationship with God

I grew up Catholic in a middle class family. I was baptized in 1951 and later encouraged to go to confession, C.C.D., church and receive Holy Communion. It was very ritualistic for me EXCEPT for the time when I was nine years old and was obsessed with having a sister.

At the time I had a four year old fun-filled brother that I enjoyed. I asked my parents if they would help me get a sister. My mother had a very difficult pregnancy with my brother therefore they were less than enthusiastic, somehow I was able to pick up on some of their hesitancy so I suggested that they adopt. It was apparent to me that wasn't working either. I was determined to have a sister so I went straight to Jesus.

I had a beautiful statue of Jesus when he was resurrected on my tall bureau so I prayed very hard one glorious night! I strongly felt Jesus' presence in the room and proceeded to ask Him that if He was really there to please move my area rug. Well I saw the rug move and knew then that we would be blessed with a baby girl in our family. The next morning at breakfast I was telling my mother about how I prayed to Jesus and to this day I remember the shocked look on her face. That July evening my beautiful, talented sister, Janie, was conceived and she was later born April 9, 1961.

As I approached the teenage years I was what you could call a sleeping or some times comatose Catholic. Neither religion nor relationship was a priority in my life. You would think that after the gift of my sister I would have moved forward instead of backwards in my relationship with Jesus. I continued to pray and in my thirties after being divorced I started to enthusiastically teach 6th grade C.C.D. That occurred only after going to church to pray in despair one day. I promised to teach if God would help and save my son, George, from his addictive behaviors. The years went by and I continued to teach and George's problems escalated. To make matters worse my daughter, Ann, began to exhibit bipolar behavior. I learned that God does not always answer as we expect Him to – but He always answers in ways that agree with His plan.

One May Friday night in 1992 I again turned to God and asked Him to help my children and please send me a good man. The next day my friend, Beverly, insisted that she and I go out. I reluctantly conceded and low and behold I met Carl Smith. There was instantly a powerful mutual and spiritual attraction. Carl later shared with me that the same Friday night he asked God to send him a good women.

A memorable morning in 1993 was when I was cleaning the house and fell to my knees and talked to God. I said that I was from this day forward going to live my life putting Him first. That meant that each morning I would read one chapter in the Bible and write on the side what I learned. I also wrote to God in a journal thanking Him for His blessings and praying for those in need. This precious time with Him took 15-20 minutes each morning. I have changed and matured spiritually due to this extremely valuable time in the morning.

I also realized that my job was not to go to church to receive a blessing I was to go to be a blessing. In the year 2000 I was asked to coordinate the 6th grade Religious Education Program. I was delighted to incorporate into the program Bible knowledge for the children and the teachers.

One night at C.C.D. a speaker came in and expressed to us that she also wrote to God and that He wrote back! It was at that moment that I knew that if I quieted myself and listened that God would also speak to me. Yes, God does talk to me and I write it down. Unlike me with a mouth full, what God says is extremely straight to the point and valuable. When you plug into His power source expect great things and the strength to battle the not so great things…

In 2004 I was walking the beach and asked God, "Why me, why do I have so much and some people have so little?" In the wind He answered me and said "Because I want you to share." I said, "Can you be more specific?" God said, "I will show you."

After that incident I got the message and I began to ask my friends and neighbors if they would be interested in starting a group that would raise funds to help our brothers and sisters in need. I was amazed when we had our first meeting and my dinning room chairs were full of willing and wonderful committee members. We called ourselves The Thanksgiving Guardian Angels. For seven great years we made a positive difference and then I felt that I was redirected to the Kiwanis as an avenue to share.

I was going along the path of life enjoying my marriage to Carl, my job, my volunteer work and my renewed relationship with my parents who came to live in the same town.

Suddenly in 2007 I didn't feel very well and one day sitting alone in my play room the Holy Spirit came to me and asked if I was ready to die? I said NO! I thought I must be loosing my mind and in a sense, I was. I felt a strange strong warning come over me.

My dear and only sister, Janie, who I mentioned earlier, sings in a band and I was drinking water and began coughing and Lisa, the wife of the drummer, said to my sister that she thought that I had a seizure.

I began to get curious about my health. Carl was at the computer and I asked him to look up seizure. We did and the word brain tumor came up and when we researched tumor we realized that I had many of the symptoms, therefore we went together to my doctor and an MRI showed a 5.5cm (lemon size) tumor on the right frontal lobe.

The neurologist said that it was about 4-5 weeks from redirecting the brain and snapping the brain stem…resulting in instant death. Carl and I agreed that it must be removed immediately. My sister and I named it Tommy the tumor. Thank God for bringing us some humor and the support of Janie at this crossroad. When I was about to undergo 10 hours of surgery I said to God "Do whatever You want with me I am in Your hands."

I prayed and appreciated the talented hands that would touch my brain. Two days later I held those precious hands of one my surgeons and prayed over them as he cried. It was again my relationship with GOD that helped me through the entire process, healed me and here I am five years later in good health and typing this testimony.

My prayer for you is that this book helps to strengthen your transition from religion to relationship with our God and His precious Son, Jesus...

With Love, Elaine Smith

†

I have always believed in God. As a young child, I was the only one in my family to attend the Episcopal Church in our town. I either walked to get the bus, or my dad would drive me and I would take the bus home. I sang in the choir as a child, and taught Sunday school as a teen there.

I'm not sure when it started, but I also always read my Bible before I went to bed, usually Psalms, as that was the only part I could understand. (It had been a family Bible that I found)...and I always prayed. I have memories of knowing that God was there and answering my prayers. Once, when my mother had been very ill and my sister in law was also in the hospital, I had a very severe anxiety attack which just wouldn't go away, and I remember pleading with God for help, as I just didn't know what to do, and there was no one to help me. After quite a while, it did abate, and I knew that God answered. I would have been in real trouble had he not answered that prayer. I still remember how awful that felt. It was very intense.

In high school, I was chosen the best business student in my class and had applied to attend Stenotype School in Boston to pursue being a court reporter. I had been accepted, but had a longing to become a teacher. Interestingly, a friend in high school (we both played the violin) told me she was going to attend a Christian college in the next town over from us. I had never heard of it, but it sounded good, and safe, so I ended up applying.

Through God-ordained circumstances, I was accepted, even though my mother had tried to discourage me, stating, truthfully, that they had no money to send me to college. I ended up getting many scholarships, and God had indeed paved the way. (That is also where I met my husband of now 42 years).

I heard the gospel preached at the chapel services, and even went forward in response to an altar call, but I didn't really understand what was happening, or what was supposed to happen, and nothing did. I had a "head knowledge" of salvation, but no change in my life.

Years later, when I had given birth to our first child, we were driving through Braintree, and I thought of an old family friend whom I hadn't seen for several years. I wanted to show off our new baby, or course, so we stopped by to see her. During the "getting caught up" visit, my friend mentioned that she had been "born again". Well, I knew what that was about...after all, I had attended a Christian college, so I said OK. What I couldn't understand, though, was why she kept talking about the Lord! Anyway, we enjoyed our visit and returned home.

A few weeks later, I called her to see if we could get together so she could see our new home. She answered the phone stating, "I can't talk now, I have some ladies here for prayer". Saying she would get back to me, I hung up the phone. Immediately after hanging up the phone, I knew I had to go to her house! I didn't hear a voice, I just knew. So, as quickly as I could, I gathered up my son, got into the car and started to Braintree. It was about a 30 minute drive, and I wasn't sure I had enough gas, but prayed that I would get there. I was thinking, this is crazy, I didn't know what kind of praying they were doing, but I did know my friend was Catholic, and, more importantly, I hadn't been invited! But still, I knew I had to be there, and couldn't wait to get there! When I arrived at her door, my friend welcomed me, but afterwards confessed that she thought that maybe God had just made His first mistake!

So, here I was. One of the girls took my son and kept him busy while I joined in the prayer. We sat around the dining room table, they prayed aloud, prayers unlike the Episcopal Church where you read from a prayer book. This was just "talking to God". They also sang a lot, in praise songs which were very catchy and easy to join in, so I did. It felt right. My mind kept saying, "This is crazy and uncomfortable for a staunch Episcopalian", but in my spirit, I knew it was right.

After praying and singing for a while, my friend asked if they could "pray over me". I didn't see any harm in it, so I said OK. She prayed something about being filled with the Holy Spirit, and when they finished, I KNEW who Jesus was! He had revealed Himself to me, and I was truly born again. I no longer simply had a head knowledge, He was now in my heart. I had joy, peace, and couldn't wait to share Him with others.

I experienced a very real experience with a very real God that day. My life was changed from that day on. No more doubt! I was a Christian, born again, and no one can ever take that away from me. I have since learned that one may have a "head knowledge," as I did, but never experience God. Now I know that if you keep seeking, He is faithful, and He will reveal Himself to you if you keep seeking.

Linda Benjamin, New Hampshire

✝

Bill's Story July 26, 2012

I was very insecure as a child. I'm not sure why, but I
was quite socially inept. I was not accepted well by my
peers from grade school right on up through high
school. This had a deep impact on me. Around the
time I was six, the Lord revealed Himself to my parents.
From that point onwards the Bible became the focal
point of our family. I have clear memories of Dad
reading the Bible to us after he'd come home from work
and my Mom leading a children's bible club in our
home. It wasn't too much longer before I understood
the basics of the good news – that God loved me yet
because of my sin I was separated from Him. Though I
do not remember the exact time, I placed my faith in
Jesus and believed that the punishment due me for my
sin, He took upon Himself on the cross. My sister,
brother and I placed our faith in Jesus around this same
time.

I do have clear memories of seeing Dad's Bible open on
his desk with underlines and notes. My Mom would
often sit and study scripture, filling notebooks with
insights. She would insist that we children go to our
rooms and not return until we heard God speak to us
from His Word. Thus, through their influence, I grew to
understand the significance of personally understanding
and obeying what I learned in God's Word.

The rejection from kids at school came to a crisis for me
in 1984. As a freshman in high school, I desperately
wanted to fit in and was beginning to realize that my life
in Christ was part of the problem of why I was not
accepted. I could either embrace my friends' behavior
to fit in or follow the Lord and His Word and what I

knew was right. On a December youth retreat in NH, the Lord brought me to a point of decision. God used the loneliness and lack of acceptance from my peers to drive me towards Him.

It was in these last three years of high school where the Lord really worked in my heart, helping my faith become my own versus something I blindly followed my parents in. God brought four men to pour some of their lives into mine during this time. It was from them I put feet to what I had been learning. I learned how to share Jesus with others in practical ways. I learned about releasing my bitterness towards my peers at school who were rejecting and teasing me. I realized the vast majority of the world did not understand the good news of Jesus Christ. The message was either unknown to them or adulterated through the lenses of politics and religious tradition. Though ignorant of historical perspective, I concluded that much of what I had been exposed to of "organized Christianity" had really lost much of the New Testament expression of what being a follower of Jesus really meant. Those traditions confused me but did not deter me.

Through all these events God was implanting in me a strong desire not to waste my life. The American Dream didn't appeal to me with its façade of security and safety. I wanted to make a difference. The only difference I knew that was long lasting and real could only be made possible through Jesus' activity in people's minds, hearts and lives and that was where I discovered the overarching passion in my life.

While God calls all of us to be disciple-makers no matter the career path we choose, it was during my freshman year at college when I was compelled to switch majors and pursue a course that would eventually lead me to work in South Asia, equipping the church to proclaim the life-transforming and joyful message of Jesus to Muslims. Living in South Asia now for over a decade, I'm often reminded of the foundation of God's Word laid up in my heart by my mother and father and the other men God had placed in my life. The things they passed on still cling tightly to me. The challenges of parenthood, marriage of 20 years, deadlines, finances and living and working cross-culturally all keep the foundation clear – continuing to bring my thoughts, attitudes and actions into submission to God's Word by passionately pursuing loving God and others. As my Dad often used to say, "We all come limping to the cross." I remain daily in need of the Holy Spirit's power for the challenges I face, whether it be simply for speaking to people around me with love, gentleness and humility or for being sensitive to the Spirit's guidance as I interact with South Asian Muslims who don't know Jesus as their Lord.

Most recently I have seen the Lord work in my own heart as my family has changed. My two oldest children have left home for college leaving only two at home. I did not realize to what depth this would affect me and the dynamics of our family. Yet God is helping me embrace this new chapter of family life. I am seeing God provide for them as He did for me at that age. It's an exciting adventure of faith.

†

Hebrews 2:14 & 15 (The Living Bible)

Since we God's children are human beings, made of flesh and blood, He became flesh and blood too by being born in human form; for only as a human being could He die and in dying break the power of the devil who had the power of death. Only in that way could He deliver those who *through fear of death have been living all their lives in constant dread.* (Italics and emphasis mine)

That pretty much sums up the first 30 years of my life. I was raised in the Catholic faith, went to church on Sunday, Sunday school, made my First Holy Communion, went to Religious Education, as it was called in those days and was confirmed in the faith. Occasionally my Mother would attend church with me; she had a strong faith in Mary and said that she knew that Mary walked with her hand on my Mom's shoulder. She had a huge statue of Mary in her bedroom.

I believed what I had been taught. I knew and could recite the 10 commandments and all of the prayers that were in the book. Never read a Bible.

I knew that Jesus died on the cross, that I was a sinner and nothing I did could release me from the fact that I was going to hell. You had to be "good" to go to Heaven and I wasn't!

As a child I was molested by a family member, got married at an early age and in no time had 5 children. Two of them passed away from Cystic Fibrosis. I was raped twice, once with a shotgun put to my head. Life took its toll on me and I ended up in a psychiatrist's office after two years of panic attacks and deep depression. Every time that I had a panic attack I would pray an Act of Contrition that I had been taught as a child. I knew I was going to die and go to hell. I couldn't cope with the death of my children and life as it had been.

In 1975 God occasioned that a woman would come into my life. We met at a meeting at our children's school. She was very friendly, kind, and did so many things for other people. What a "good" person she was!

Over the next 6 months or so our friendship developed. One night I attended a plant party at one of our mutual friend's home. There were a lot of Catholic ladies there and the conversation somehow got around to trying to be a "good" person. My friend said, "You can be a good person all of your life and still go straight to hell! It was as though someone set off a bomb in the room. Silence is very loud!

Now I knew that what she said wasn't true and a few days later I told her so. She said that she knew that she was going to Heaven. I knew she was going to Heaven because she was a "good" person and did "good" things. She shared the Gospel with me, prayed with me and gave me a Bible and a little booklet called The Day the King's Son Died. I went home.

I didn't read the Bible, it had too many pages, but I did read the booklet. At the end of the booklet there was a prayer. I prayed it with every part of my being and by the end of it I was born again, cleansed, forgiven, accepted in the Beloved and I knew it!!! I knew that Jesus was alive, He was real, He would never leave me, He loved me and I was going to spend eternity with Him in Heaven.

I went back to my psychiatrist and told her that I didn't need her anymore because I had Jesus. She said, "You are right, you don't need me anymore". I got rid of the pills that I had been taking for the panic attacks right after I felt a twinge of fear coming on. I knew that the enemy would use them against me and tempt me to fear and not trust Jesus.

I had not been able to drive my car in over a year and I began to drive again. I was no longer afraid to be far from home. My language literally cleaned up over night. The sins that I had been so engrossed in no longer held any grip on me. I was set free from alcoholism. It ran ramped through my family and in fact my Mom died from it at the age of 56.

With my limited knowledge of the scriptures I began sharing what I did know about Jesus with everyone around me.

Some believed and were saved, others didn't.

Life didn't remain as perfect as it was in those days. I have had some more hard lessons to learn, sins to confess, and how to trust Jesus with all of it. I tried to walk away from Him for about 6 years but He never gave up on me and brought me back close to Him again. Now I will forever praise Him. He is Faithful, He is Love, He is Mercy, He is Grace, and He is all that we need.

Carole MacDonald - Florida

†

After around twelve years of playing
Christian because of a prayer I had said in
front of the television in 77 and making the
phone call to the number on the screen and
after having read the Bible cover to cover
around three times, and journaling thousands
of pages and having acted the fool in front
of hundreds of people over the course of
around 10 years and being jailed, and being
labeled manic depressive and forced by law
enforcement to take lithium, and living as a
homeless person scrounging out of
dumpsters one day and earning $150.00 the
next, and getting drunk, and smoking pot,
and using women, and following after every
illicit thought that ran through my mind, and
having my heart broken many times and
breaking a few myself and being beaten till
almost dead or at least having felt like I had
died and that several times, after fighting
physically for other people's rights and
being beaten again, after cursing God, and
never being grateful and after being stabbed
in the throat and living when for all intents
and purposes I shouldn't have..............
after all that and more.......................

I asked God while driving down a road in Massachusetts - IS THIS JESUS FOR REAL?

I was looking through the windshield of some vehicle I was driving with a Bible beside me in the seat and a clear audible voice told me to read John 3:14. Without missing a beat I opened my Bible and read; "Just as Moses lifted up the serpent on the pole in the desert so must the Son of Man be lifted up."

By Gods infinite mercy and grace I knew the story well from Numbers 21 verses 5-9. Israel was complaining against God and Moses as I had complained my whole life against God and any authority that He had ever placed over me and against any good thing He had ever given me. So God sent fiery serpents into the camp, they bit the people and people began to die. Then they turned to Moses and asked him to pray, he did and God told him to make a brass snake and put it on a pole and that anyone who looked on it would be healed.

Then and there I knew in my heart that death was required, at first I thought it meant I would have to die through persecution or such, as time went on the Holy Spirit made

it very clear that I needed to look to this
Jesus to be saved.

Only God could take all the shattered shards
of this my life and do anything with it. So
He fired up the pieces turning them into
liquid and He being the potter is still
molding the clay to this day. Come, Lord
Jesus, come.

Persecution did follow in many ways but for
that I am very glad. Not for the persecution
but because now I know that my name is
written in the Lamb's Book of Life because
of Jesus' sacrifice, His death, burial and
resurrection. I thank You, our God and our
Lord Jesus Christ, for counting me worthy to
have suffered very much for the cross of
Jesus Christ.. As of right now I cannot
know the rewards I have waiting for me but
He is gracious in saving such a sinner as
myself and that, in and of itself is enough.
Now except for my own thorn in the flesh,
as Paul, because of the many visions and the
multitude of them I am very buffeted daily
to keep me from way too much pride.

Jesus Christ of Nazareth is my all in all,
What can man do to me? My hope is in the
resurrection of the dead in Christ and to
walk the streets of gold praising His holy

name. I Thessalonians 4 verse 16-18 "For the Lord Himself shall descend from heaven with a shout, with the voice of the archangel, and with the trump of God: and the dead in Christ shall rise first: Then we which are alive and remain shall be caught up together with them in the clouds, to meet the Lord in the air: and so shall we ever be with the Lord. Wherefore comfort one another with these words."

Amen and amen and amen and amen and amen. Can ya tell I am happy yet? What Satan has meant for evil God has turned into gold and pure gold it is.

Jim MacDonald - Florida

†

My Life with Jesus

We have many ways to describe how we come to believe in Christ: 'born again', 'saved', 'came to Christ,' 'asked Jesus into my heart', etc. I have used these phrases to communicate what happened to me when I became a Christian, because they are well known. However, to describe what really happened, I would say I came to a very deep conviction and knowledge that Jesus really is the Son of God, and that He rose again from the dead. Then, as I realized those two truths, one single thought became very clear: all my next steps in life would be based on them.

The practical way this happened, of course, had a lot to do with people and circumstances. Two high school friends were Christians and they influenced me. Also, I found, one day, perfectly 'by accident', C.S. Lewis' well-known book *Mere Christianity* while browsing the shelves in our state library. I had never heard of him before, but as I read the book, I thought, "This really is true; I always thought it was."

I had just graduated from college and was working when I found this book. Around that time I also decided to travel to Europe. I had vague goals but had studied German and so off I went. One of my Christian friends arranged that I could work at a Christian Youth Hostel in Amsterdam. That was my next significant step, as I walked literally out of the darkness one night into the light of this hostel and the staff there. I clearly remember the light in the face of the fellow who came to greet me as I walked through the door.

After that, I became a Christian by imitation. I wasn't opposed to the idea, and wanted whatever it was they had. The short version is that they prayed and read their Bible, so I started to do the same. I also read a book about having a 'quiet time' and started doing that every morning. Gradually things began to change in me and over the course of the year I stayed there I entered into my new life in Christ! That's how it happened for me.

Now, 37 years later, the most important thing in my life which keeps me on track with the Lord is still the same. It's absolutely essential that I spend time daily with Him in prayer, meditation, and Scripture reading and study. We grow, we learn, we stumble, and just continue with the work He begun as He likewise continues working in and with us.

Joan – Pennsylvania

†

I grew up a good Catholic child, got baptized
(although not my choice at the time), made first
Communion, went to Confession, and got
confirmed all while going to a Catholic school from
grade 1-8.

Looking back I spent all those years being around
other Catholics and trying to be a good kid.... but
never heard about having a relationship with Jesus
or even being encouraged to read the Bible.

It wasn't until several years later when I was in high
school that my mother, who was also a Catholic,
found Jesus, became born again and had a
relationship with Him, that I heard about how I was
a sinner (even though I was a good Catholic kid)
and needed to be forgiven. Seeds planted.......

In the mean time my mother was telling everyone
about Jesus and a lot of my aunts and uncles
became Christians and had that relationship with
Jesus and I saw and heard from them the message
again. Seeds watered......

I was invited to a Full Gospel Business Men's
breakfast and accepted Jesus as my Savoir and
became born again! Seeds growing......

I spent a lot of years as a young adult in different
denomination churches that were preaching the full
gospel and growing as a Christian. I was baptized
by submersion in water as an outward sign of my
being born again. (this was my decision) Seeds
growing.....

I also spent a lot of years dealing with great struggles and feeling like I let Jesus down on a number of the battles I had lost.....however, thanks to the Word of God, and His promises and faithfulness I was able to recommit to Jesus and continue on! Seeds growing....

Through that time I went through a divorce and that was unfortunate; however, I was blessed with three beautiful girls who have grown into beautiful young adults and I thank God for them!

I met a nice Catholic girl and we started dating, she was like me growing up... trying to be nice and doing good.   Over time I witnessed to her as much as I felt God gave me an opportunity.   Seeds planted...

One day we had a talk about a Buddha statue she gave me, it was her grandfather's and it meant a lot to her. (I had thrown the statue out and did not tell her). In the discussion I explained why I threw it out.... It represented a god, and for me, I wanted no other gods above my God. She listened and understood.   Seeds watered....

I was blessed the day she came to me and wanted to pray to accept Jesus as her savior!   Seeds growing....

We got married and had a beautiful baby girl! Today we attend a great Nazarene church where the gospel is preached.

I have a beautiful wife, 4 beautiful girls, 2 beautiful grandchildren: a grandson and a granddaughter! I thank God for them!

GOD IS FAITHFUL!

Dennis Campbell – Massachusetts

†

My Testimony-Denise Campbell

Having grown up in a strict Catholic family, I
followed the old school rules my parents learned
and passed on down to me from their parents. We
went to church every Sunday, attended CCD, made
sure all the sacraments were completed on time,
went to confession, said the rosary, and prayed only
the Lord's Prayer, the Hail Mary and Glory be. The
Act of Contrition was in there somewhere too. But
never was the Bible mentioned or learning God's
Word. I thought I was a "good Catholic" and had
God in my life, but I guess I had no idea what that
really meant. And I never felt that God was there
for me. I thought I'd meet him when I got to
Heaven, if I got to Heaven and that would be that.

As an adult I really did not attend church much. I
never felt like I was getting much out of it. It was
always the same old memorized words, sitting,
kneeling, standing like robots, with a gloomy
feeling and never really walking away with
anything significant, except a communion snack
signaling the end of the Mass was near.

When I got married, (the 1st time) there was no
other option but to be married in our Catholic
Church. Although the person I was marrying was
Catholic and had been baptized and had his First
Communion, he had not been confirmed. So getting
confirmed became necessary along with the pre-
Cana classes that were required for us to be married.
So with all the requirements completed, we were
allowed to be married in my parents' Catholic

Church, by their priest, which was very important to them, not so much to us.

Fast forward a few years and divorce is upon me with heartbreak, embarrassment and disappointment for not only me, but my family and our family priest. Before the legalities of divorce were even close to being final, I was being bombarded with pressure to start the Catholic annulment process. The pressure was tremendous and not something I was prepared to start or emotionally ready to reveal to the total strangers that would be reading the intimate details of such a significant and personal heartbreak in my life and deciding if it was OK for me to be annulled in God's eyes and allowed to receive Communion again and be a proper practicing Catholic with all that erased from my past and I could be "virginized" again. None of it felt right to me.

Upon seeking outside support, I joined a Divorce Support Group that was held in a very different church. Everyone had their own divorce story, but they also talked about "being saved" which I did not understand. The term "born again" was spoken about on occasion and I thought I was attending "one of those" churches where fanatical born again Christians lived. They were by no means Catholic and the whole experience was not what I was brought up to believe was right. When I spoke to my parents about the support group, they were very nervous about the church and what I was getting myself into and reluctant for me to attend. They preferred me to speak to our family priest, which I did, and he only discussed the annulment process and how he did not see this coming. In looking back to the pre-Cana and what he saw and experienced working with the engaged couple we were in front of him, the surprise he spoke of really wasn't surprising, but that's a whole other story.

I did get support from this Divorce Support Group and met some wonderful people, so I went back and continued doing so for a while. I kept at a distance religiously from them, but became closer supporting each other with the similar experiences we were all going through at that time. When that group session ended, I never went back, but I guess in the back of my mind I had stored much of what they said about being saved and wondered what they meant.

Fast forward a bit longer and I meet a wonderful man that I begin dating and now for many years that I am proud and blessed to be married to and share a wonderful family with. In the beginning, he never talked about being saved or born again, but I held in my mind that he had gone to a Catholic Middle School, so thought that was ok.

Through our relationship and meeting his family, we attended a Dedication, which was so foreign to me, but seemed like what I knew Baptism to be. He explained the difference between the choice of baptism and when parents and family dedicate to bring the baby up to know God and teach them to have a relationship with Him.

We also had a situation where he had the opportunity to bring idolatry to my attention. Although I did not have any other idols, it was important to recognize what things around me might be seen as idols and be inappropriate in

God's eyes. I also started to notice in his church there was just a cross, not a crucifix which was very different than the Catholic Church and the whole feel of the service with the upbeat praise music and energy of people truly loving God filled the air. Never had I seen that before. These differences really caught my attention. It felt so good.

When I met his mother, she had Bibles all over the place. She talked to me about the Word of God and praying and was always referring to different Bible verses. She had so many miracle stories about how God helped her through difficult times in her life. She kept saying to me "talk to Him! All you need to do is talk to Him! He is there for you!" She also explained that knowing the Bible and reading it daily would help God guide me through my life. I couldn't believe how much writing there was in her Bible and highlighting verses with dates and notes and names.

This special lady also prayed with me very late at night on the phone during a few times of emotional need when she hardly knew me. She kept encouraging me to ask God to come into my heart and accept Jesus as my savior and start my own relationship with Him. All of this was very out of my comfort zone, but was also so inviting at the same time.

This all was bringing me back to that Divorce Support Group and reminded me of many of the things they had said in our group sessions. Only the encouragement coming from this special man and his mother felt like a safer source to accept exploring a different type of way with God. A relationship which I knew nothing about or how to even start.

As time passed I kept an open mind and struggled with how to start and tried to read the Bible. I had asked my mother if she ever read the Bible and her response to me was, "No, we were always told not to. That it was too confusing and that the priest was the one who should interpret it for you." Again it was very discouraging for me to get started.

Finally I spoke to this special man and asked him "How do I go about this?" He told me "It's very simple. You say a prayer for Jesus to come into your heart, tell Him you accept Him as your personal savior and you want Him to guide your life, that's it." It sounded so easy. So hard to believe that was it. All of the joy and content I saw in others that I longed for came from just that? I wondered if my world was going flip upside down and change from that moment forward and I would feel it all over. I wanted it. I asked him to pray the prayer with me. We did. My world did not flip upside down at that moment. I questioned whether or not I said it right. Was it true? Why everything didn't change at that moment. I kept looking for signs shortly after that prayer. Big signs. Nothing.

So, we were preparing for a weekend trip up to Bar Harbor with his 3 daughters to visit his aunt who was very sick. Before we left I asked him how this really happened and if it wasn't happening to me, that I felt like such a child and I was starting from scratch at an adult age to have a relationship with my God who has known me all along. How was I going to do this! I needed God to speak to me like a

child so I understand what is going on. He
encouraged me to tell God that and said that's how
everyone starts, no matter what age you are. You
mature as you grow in your faith, but right now
you're an infant. It's OK to ask Him to speak to
you like a child if that's what you need. So I did. I
thought a lot about that on the trip up to Bar Harbor.

So there we are in the hotel room getting ready to
head over to his aunt's house. 4 girls, 1 bathroom
…it took some time. The TV was on and a cartoon
kid's show was playing. The characters in the show
broke it down very simply for me as I was
watching. "Jesus died for our sins and if we believe
that we can be with Him in Heaven."

It hit me like a ton of bricks. I looked up, laughed
and thanked God for that. I was looking way too
much into it. It truly was that simple. When I
asked Him simply what I needed, He answered my
prayer. And that is when my life began to change.

I began talking to God, telling Him my fears and
feelings and asked for His help to make decisions in
my life that I did not know how to handle. For the
first time in my life I put things in God's hands and
did not worry afterward.

He showed me the way. I look back at all the seeds
He planted to lead me to where I was and knew that
all I had gone through was in His plan for MY life.

I also learned that as my life proceeded and my
relationship progressed with God, it was a two-way
street and I needed to be open to talking to Him and
listening and most importantly to be patient and

wait on His direction. I found He is so faithful and forgiving. My husband would encourage me to talk to God and ask Him for direction and share my desires and hopes with Him so He could lead me along the way. No matter how silly it felt to me, God cared about all my feelings. So I really set myself free and opened myself up honestly to Him about everything.

He became the center of my life, my go-to Person to talk to. He is the center of my marriage which would be difficult without Him. He led me to understand and know for certain a child would bless our marriage and it was His will. A thought I struggled with for years.

My life with God is now a relationship. I don't just have God in my life as a religion as I had for many years. I have Him as a friend, a confidant, a counselor, a forgiver Who guides me along the path He has for me. I long to be on this path and have His will be done in my life. It feels so good to feel so safe knowing that He is in control and I just let go and do my part to read His Word, look for His guidance and share it all with others.

It's an amazing personal relationship that I did not understand could exist for me and anyone one else who chooses to have it. Now I know that it is still and always will be a growing process as I go.

†

Testimony of Amy Fulton

As I look back over the years that I have been a Christian, I can see my walk with God has been in numerous stages or phases.

Phase one was when I first heard about Jesus from my mother when I was about 7 or 8 years old. My parents had both become Christians and my mother began reading the Bible with my brothers and me, telling us about Jesus; about His birth, death and resurrection, and why He died for us.

Somehow I knew even at a young age that what she was saying was true. I remember praying with her and my brothers, acknowledging that I was a sinner and that I needed Jesus to come into my life. However, I think because of my age, my motivation was not of repentance for sin, but of fear of going to hell. I did not and could not fully comprehend just who Jesus was and what being a Christian meant. Daily my mother made sure I would read my Bible and listen to see if God had anything to say to me and encouraged my walk with Jesus.

The second phase of my walk was in the years that followed when I learned to believe what I did, not on the faith of my parents but as an individual. In my early teens, I began questioning just why I believed what I did. Along with becoming involved in many youth groups over the years, I would attend different denominations of church services with my parents. It was at one of these services that I heard a speaker encourage people who had accepted Christ to make a public acknowledgement of it by coming to the front of the church.

Although I had heard pastors and speakers say this before, I had never felt the need to do so until that time. I was at a point in my life when I was truly questioning my Christianity and wanted to recommit my life to the Lord. I remember walking to the front of the church with tears streaming down my eyes with every intention of deepening my walk with the Lord.

However as time when on, I went to college, began working, and was married. My Christian walk was put aside as my responsibilities increased and eventually took over my life. I knew in the back of my mind that my relationship with Jesus was lacking and that I was feeling the result of it in every aspect of my life. For whatever reason, I was not ready to open my life and say "Lord, work in me and use me."

As the years went by, my physical and emotional state at times were such that I am fully aware that had I not turned to Jesus when I did, I would not be alive today.

The third phase of my walk began when I became pregnant with my first child. For medical reasons I quit my job and suddenly had a lot of time on my hands. After the first few months at home I knew I had to begin paying attention to my relationship with Jesus, which up until that point had been almost non-existent. I began attending a fellowship called Isaiah 58 Women's Fellowship, based on the book of Isaiah in the Bible and the 58th Chapter. Their premise was to be "…women who believe God has called us to re-evaluate our lives … to be repairers of the breach …to bring mercy and not judgment to His hurting people … We have decided Jesus is more important than our own hopes, dreams, goals, expectations and desires."

There is more to it than that, but those words struck a cord in me. I knew I was at a crossroads in my life and needed to really begin walking with the Lord, not just for myself, but for my marriage and for my coming child, otherwise I could not be the woman, wife or mother I knew God wanted me to be. At one of the meetings, we all felt the Lord was saying to us "Will you let Me use your hands?" It was at this time I made a conscious decision to open my life to whatever God wanted for me, whether it was to do a work in me or to use me to help someone else. I began praying regularly, reading my Bible, and spending real time with Jesus.

Once I made myself available to God, it was as if my eyes had been closed and were now open. I could see myself growing spiritually by leaps and bounds. My walk was made even deeper after I had my first child and found myself exhausted and completely in unfamiliar territory. I quickly found that being a mother is a learning experience. When Marijke would cry I would try to sing to her, but since I did not know any lullabies, I borrowed a hymnbook from my aunt and began singing the praise songs that we sing in church. I found myself not just singing these songs to soothe Marijke, but would sing them as praises to Jesus while comforting our daughter at the same time. I know that this was a catalyst for a spiritual awakening in me and for my allowing the Holy Spirit to work in me.

After our second daughter, Micaela, was born, I again took another look at my life. We had been attending the church my husband had gone to for years, South Shore Baptist Church in Hingham, MA. He was a member of the church, but I had not yet made a commitment to any "religion" or religious beliefs. My faith was one of a Biblically-based personal relationship with Jesus rather than a following of rules and regulations. I also realized, however, that my husband and I needed to be "spiritually evenly yoked." I wanted us to be able to present a united front to our girls as they grew up, not just physically and emotionally but also spiritually. To this end, I felt God telling me to become a member of SSBC, which I did in 1998.

By 2000 my faith had been tested to what I thought were my limits. My husband contracted Lyme Disease and almost died numerous times. We found ourselves more than once asking God why He allowed this to happen. People would say, "We're praying for you." I remember at one point thinking, "Well thank you, but what are you praying? What if people prayed that God would heal my husband and then he died? Does that mean God did not answer the prayer? If we DON'T pray and Tim gets better, does that mean prayer doesn't mean anything?" Through much prayer and discussing this with Tim, I came to realize that when I pray for someone it is in the hope that God would be graceful and heal that person, but more that God would let that person KNOW that HE is with them and will give him/her His Grace and Strength to get through what our cursed, fragile bodies are subjected to and to help them turn to Him through it. We were very blessed in that God did answer our prayers – Tim is alive and well with only minor damage caused by the Lyme Disease.

The testing of the metal of my faith was not yet finished, however. The same day Tim was cleared to go back to work by his doctor, I had to see my doctor for excruciating pain in my lower back and legs. As of the date I am writing this, it has been 12 years since that doctor visit, and I still experience back/leg pain of varying levels every day. Sometimes it is so bad I literally scream; other times I can live a somewhat "normal" life…. But MY version of normal is quite different than the average person's. I live on pain pills but continue to try to strengthen my muscles in an effort to regain what I have lost being off my feet for most of the last decade. It became evident quite quickly at the onset of my "physical issues" that God was teaching me to lean on Him and turn to Him, and in doing so He has made me able to be there for so many other people who are hurting physically. I have been able to encourage others (Christians or not) and pray for them solely because I can relate to what they are feeling physically and emotionally… and sometimes in turn remind ME to go to Him when I am overwhelmed. Even though I HATE being in pain all the time, I have learned to actually *thank* God for allowing me to go through this so that I can use my experience with pain as a catalyst to help others turn to Him. I have also learned that when we open ourselves up to what God has for us and/or to do for Him, it is not always in a way that we would want!

I have continued to make myself available to the Lord and although I have seen the fruit of what my obedience to God and allowing Him to use me has done, I know God is not finished by any means with the work He is doing in me and through me.

†

My Christian life has been one of growth, not amazing transformation. I came to believe in Christ at a very young age. My mother made me read scripture as a child, and I believed in Christ because of what I read in scripture with a knowledge that I cannot define, I recognized that what I read was true. I decided to read the book of John and I read in John 3:16, "For God so loved the world, that he gave his only begotten Son, that whosoever believeth in him should not perish, but have everlasting life." When I read it I knew it was true and applied to me. I recognized and accepted that all men sin, that I was a child but it still meant me, I was a sinner, that sin requires payment/sacrifice, and that this sacrifice is needed to get back into acceptance before our Creator. That the sacrifice is Christ –His life, death and resurrection, and in order to receive it, one must believe in Jesus. I did not believe because it would please my parents, because my mother told me to, or because it was the family "religion". I believed because it was truth.

After this belief I went from understanding that I was a sinner to knowing I was forgiven and then on to understanding that as a saved person God had a plan, purpose, and goal for me. He wants me to grow as a person to be more like Christ. The difference before and after Christ has been purpose. I recognize I have purpose from my Creator.

Before I was saved I really didn't do many things wrong, but I recognize that I did do bad. I was an 8 year old young man, and I knew I had sinned. From my parents I knew that there was good and bad, and sometimes I failed in doing good. I had just come to recognize that there was a God – something bigger than just my family, a higher authority than any other, and I accepted this fact and the truth of Jesus.

As Christ said in John 16:33, and as Paul said in Hebrews my life has been full of suffering which to many may be small suffering, but the end result of this suffering has helped me to grow as a person towards Christ likeness. This growth has been greatest when I would invest my life in others through serving in church through serving others through being a part of society bearing in mind my directive from Christ's example - to love my neighbor, to tell them of the hope that is in me.

I encouraged anyone and everyone who wants to know about God or is a Christian to read the Bible. Read it from beginning to end, don't make any assumptions or judgments until you read the entire thing. If God is real, ask Him to show you His realness in scripture, if He is not real, then you have not wasted your time because you have read a good piece of world history… No loss. It took me about 5 years to read through the whole Bible while I was in college – yes, it took me a long time to get through college - one of my life sufferings. I had read small portions, chapters, individual books before I was in college, but I had not read through the whole Bible from beginning to end. I would read three chapters a night. One chapter of Psalms, one of Proverbs and one going through the whole Bible, repeating Psalms and Proverbs each time I completed them. Reading the entire Bible helped me understand what God wanted from His people and what I should be doing as a person. That He had a purpose in His direction and actions with humanity. History may record a lot of change in society, but God's purpose has always been the same – to communicate with His creation – us.

As I was growing up my family bounced around between different Christian churches from Catholic to Protestant denominations of all types. In each church I would find people that appeared to believe in God and those whose lives did not show that they believed, even though they went to church, and I realized that God has a plan and purpose in these different churches, because as a people we are all different. The ceremony of some churches helps some to believe, and the free spirit in other churches helps others to believe, but there is the same God: Father, Son, and Holy Spirit.

After I believed in Jesus, and went through the emotional roller coaster of the teenage years and on into adulthood, my Christian life was and continues to be one of growth. Sometimes a success and sometimes a failure, learning what is right and wrong in each intricate detail of life. Failing to do what God wants and then doing what God wants, and finding out more as I read the Bible and following different paths and falling into the problems that come into everyone's life. Dealing with frustration over life or my own failure, or not dealing with it and getting angry at people or angry at my situation, angry about things around me instead of trusting in God, and at times actually learning to trust in God and saying "Okay God, You are King of everything, You own all that there is, so

I'll trust You to take care of the situation that I'm in, and I will do what I believe is right in Your eyes. But give me wisdom because I'm just a stupid human and as Your Word says – "like the flower on the grass that is here today and gone tomorrow."

The main difference between being a Christian and not being a Christian is purpose. When I act, when I involve myself in others, when I go to church and become part of the fellowship of the believers, when I assist in ministries such as Sunday school, when I involve my life in the lives of others, when I open my mouth and talk about the hope that is in me – salvation through Jesus, and I live my belief by getting "out of my shell" or "off of my island" and involve myself with others with love, I experience growth, I experienced the peace of God. When I do right, little things happen in my life that can only be explained as a smile from God directly showing me that I'm doing the right thing. An acquaintance of mine wrote a book called *Knowing His Way*, it is a fabulous book that describes the normal trials of life, faith in God that a family clings to through each life circumstance, and how God shows His mercy and acts miraculously for His own glory. In this book the author encourages people to journal their prayer life and the answers to prayer. It is a great reminder of the reality of God in our daily living.

As I read God's Word and fill my mind with the Bible I recognize more and more what God wants me to do as a person - to get involved. This is the exact opposite of the "lessons" of this world, of media, of entertainment. Instead of living life for self fulfillment, I need to live my life fulfilling the responsibilities that God has placed in my life:

- Keeping busy with work - *1 Thessalonians 4:11 ... make it your ambition to lead a quiet life and attend to your own business and work with your hands...*
- Providing for my family - *1 Timothy 5:8 Anyone who does not provide for their relatives, and especially for their own household, has denied the faith and is worse than an unbeliever.*
- Attending church services to give and receive encouragement - *Hebrews 10:25 ...not forsaking our own assembling together, as is the habit of some, but encouraging one another; and all the more as you see the day drawing near.*
- Loving God and people - *Mark 12:30-31 'Love the Lord your God with all your heart and with all your soul and with all your mind and with all your strength.' The second is this: 'Love your neighbor as yourself.' There is no commandment greater than these.*

When I fail to recognize God as Lord of my life, and I start to follow my own will instead of the direction I know God would have me follow, I find myself falling into despair because of the suffering in the world and pointlessness of self fulfillment. But as I recognize Christianity in every step of my life, I have peace and comfort in God's plan and promises.

John16.33 "I have told you these things so that in Me you may have peace. You will have suffering in this world. Be courageous! I have conquered the world."

Even in suffering, there is purpose and peace in God. More is written on suffering in Hebrews chapter 12 and 13, in James 1:2-8, and 2 Corinthians 4, but what has been most evident in all of my reading is that God wants me to live with courageous confidence as I follow him.

When I bend with the wind in the direction that I believe God is pushing I have peace in my heart, I have peace in my soul, I have contentment, and I recognize hope in my life. I have a purpose.

Bob van den Akker – Mesa, Arizona

†

The hand of God at work: testimony of
Khiengchai Fulton

I was born in Laos, a small country on the
border of Thailand. I grew up going to the
temple, memorizing Buddhist prayers, and
giving alms to the Buddhist monks two
times a day. In our home, we had this statue
of Buddha that all of us would pray to. At
night, we would do our school work, eat
dinner, and before heading to bed, we would
bow down three times to the statue and sing
our memorized chant.

My father was a government official so we
were doing well. Then life started to change.
The political situation became unsettled
when the communists took over. Some of
the former political leaders were taken to
prison. My father was not safe. He had been
sent to prison three times already.

As a young child, I knew little of what was
going on. We knew that people were
escaping to other countries. I knew that it
was dangerous and very illegal to flee from
Laos. In God's mercy, my father arranged
for us to go on a "vacation." In our culture,
nobody goes on vacation. We left nearly

everything behind, saying no good-byes to family and friends.

My dad had incredible connections from being a politician. He knew where the safest crossing was. He knew whose house would host the eleven of us. The secrecy of this event must be secure. Our friends must sacrifice their own life so we can escape to freedom. The consequences if caught would likely be prison. Or death.

There are couple memories that I can recall of our escape. One is that my mother put dirt on our entire forehead and prayed over all of us. My next recollection was that when we got across another river, there was a man waiting for us. We were in the jungle in Thailand. We walked along a tropical path and entered a hut. There on the floor of this hut, a family had a meal waiting for our family. This is God's hand. Our goal was to live – not shot escaping. But here we are in a hut with a meal prepared for us. Here we were getting across with someone to welcome us with a meal.

We arrived in a Thai refugee camp with no problems. Our time there was good. Refugee camps are nothing glorious as most people tried to maintain normalcy and stay alive.

Not so with my parents. Even in the most depressing place, my mother and father were able to get work. My father was able to get a job with the Catholic Church. At this church my sisters and I were able to take dance lessons, got baptized and learned French. My mom started her own small business. She would get up early and get vegetables from outside the camp. She would bring them into camp and resell for a higher price. We were able to have fruit and veggies due to this business.

Our whole family was hoping to go to France but that door was firmly shut. France was not accepting any more refugees. That was not in God's plan. We had to spend eight months in a refugee camp. Now it is clear why God shut that door as in Rochester, MN, there were men and women who loved the Lord already preparing their hearts and homes to receive our family.

As a child, I thought it was magic when we arrived in Rochester in November 1980. It was very cold. People met us at the airport and took us home. I wondered why they offered to have eleven of us live in their home. Why did they buy us snow boots and feed us? They taught us English and brought us to church. I now know that it was because they loved the Lord Jesus and their actions matched their faith.

We were then safe and starting a new life in Rochester, Minnesota. In 1980, there were not many Laotians in Rochester, MN. Our family had to start over. We did not speak English. My dad didn't hold high political position. It was cold outside and this new life was very hard for my parents.

After one year, our family moved to Fort Smith, Arkansas. I had no idea where we were going. It was a poor southern city but lots of Laotian immigrants had relocated there. One reason that there are so many Laotians is that there was a chicken factory in a nearby town. The work was hard as both of my parents worked in a chicken processing plant. We were quite poor. We lived in an apartment with all the other Laotians. There were 8 of us in one bedroom apartment. (Our three cousins who left Laos with us were no longer with us – two moved to California and one to Florida.)

Despite the hardships, I have great memories from this part of my life. The hand of God was at work intervening again. During this poor time in our family, a Baptist church asked if my sisters and I would like to attend their private school. They will cover all tuition, books and someone will pick us up for school. I remember taking Bible classes. I remember studying about creation. I remember praying before classes. How can this be? We weren't believers. Here God orchestrated for me to go to a Christian school.

Several years later, both of my parents became very ill. My mom's upper body was covered with bumps. My father's legs became swollen to a point that he could not walk. Our friends drove us back to Minnesota. Back in Rochester, our friends bought a house for us to rent from them. Here we were again, destitute.

More tests for my mom revealed that she had cancer. She didn't have long to live - maybe nine months...at best one year. My mother died less than a year after being diagnosed with cancer. There were we, six young children with the youngest being four. At the same time my father's one kidney began to fail. He only weighed 85 pounds and needed a kidney transplant fast or he too would die.

What would happen to us? We would be orphans. Some people had volunteered to split us up. This was not good as we would have to be separated. In 3 days, my father got the kidney with a perfect match and the surgery was a success and our family was able to remain together. Thirty years later my father still has the same kidney.

God's hand was at work in Laos some 30 years ago and continues now. After high school, I went on to a Christian college and later volunteered in the Peace Corps in West Africa. I met my husband, Joe, in Niger, West Africa, and we got married in Rochester, Minnesota, in 1997.

When I read about Mary and Joseph fleeing to Egypt in the night, it brought back memories of what our family went through. Escaping at night, leaving all behind and going into the unknown countries is frightening. But God does not make mistakes. He ordains our steps.

I used to wonder why all these things happened to our family. It is clearer looking back on my 30 years of life. Through the high school ministry at our church I learned what it meant to follow Jesus 100%. At Bible camp in summer, I started my relationship with Jesus as my Lord and Savior. Through my learning about the true

God who created the Heavens and the earth, I learned that I didn't need to worship statues of Buddha and hope for the best in life. I now see how God was at work so many years ago. He loved our family long before we even knew Him or worshipped Him. All the things that I thought were very bad at the time turned out to be a way for the Lord to reach us. Since there are very few Christians in Laos, had we not fled as refugees, it is highly unlikely that I would have heard about salvation through Jesus.

Through the ministry of many believers, we learned about worshipping the one true God. Now with five of our own children, I want them to understand how faithful God is even in the most difficult and bitter of times. His hand is always at work ordaining the best for us. I am ever comforted that I have a faithful, gracious, wonderful, precious God.

†

I remember growing up with all the turmoil going on in my house, there never seemed to be peace. Now I serve the Prince of Peace. I grew up the oldest of nine with a mother who was an alcoholic and who also came from a family of turmoil.

I was a former epileptic and my mother was always worried that the next punch or bang of my head would bring on seizures that I hadn't had since I was nine years old. As a result she taught me to always be afraid, to run away from trouble if possible. So I did. But as you can imagine, I was the boy all other boys looked to pick on. I was always scared and running. I was Forest Gump before there was Forest Gump. I wasn't the fastest kid around, but I learned to run fast enough.

My father was out of the picture when I was young and he was not a nice guy. My mother made things worse by marrying my stepfather who was just as bad and probably much worse.

So many things happened that I can't share because this is going into a book which will be made available to the public. I can tell you both my father and my stepfather beat my mother. No woman deserves to get beaten, but she knew who they were and what they were capable of and would do, but in her drunkenness would egg them on. We, as kids, always tried to get in the way, but were never really able to do that.

I remember being in my teens and wondering, would things ever get any better. I was an altar boy. I know growing up I always talked about being a priest. Isn't it interesting the Bible says "We are a priestly people".

I ended up getting married in 1974 and with my new son and wife, followed my stepfather and 4 younger brothers & sisters out to California.

I ended with only one real friend the 2 1/2 years I was out there. His parents invited us to their church, which met in a school on Sundays. I remember an altar call and going up and receiving Jesus. They gave me a Bible and I started reading not really understanding what happened. But as I continued to read, I started to draw closer to the Lord. One night, when I was in bed with my wife asleep, I was suddenly awakened. It was Jesus. He said, "Don, I know everything you've done in your life and everything you are going to do, but I want you to tell everyone that I (Jesus) am the answer they are looking for. I'm the solution to their problems."

As you can guess, I never even heard of anything like this before. I woke my wife up and asked if she heard anything and she said no she was asleep. I told her the next morning and then I told my friend's parents. They said I should tell the Pastor. I did. He said we all want to feel so close to God that sometimes we imagine we actually hear His voice. I was discouraged, but I knew what I heard.

I fell into financial difficulty and friends and family raised money for me and my family to come home to Massachusetts in 1977. I showed God how happy I was by being best man at a friend's wedding and getting drunk for three days.

It's been an up and down walk always because of my lack of trust and walking faithfully with God. My wife and I got divorced and I have been divorced 3 times.

One thing I have learned is that God is always faithful, even when I'm not.

In 2005 God moved and got me in touch with my present wife, Jackie. We had known each other since 1980. We were both married but to different people. We were best friends both trying to serve God. She was a new Christian and God used me to help mentor her through some difficult challenges.

We lost touch in 1992. I moved to Bolton after my marriage to my second wife ended as she was cheating on me. I had given her several chances to stop but she didn't and I couldn't deal with it any longer. Meanwhile Jackie had problems with her husband and they split up. For 13 years we had no contact with each other. I was working at a place called United Funding, a mortgage refinancing call center. Jackie had just moved into an in-law attached to her daughter's home and with a new phone number that was listed to the old owner.

One evening one of my telemarketers called the number at Jackie's house. The phone rang several times before she was able to answer. When she hit the button it was as if she was placing a call which I ended up answering. We knew God had engineered it as it was way too strange to be anything else. The rest is history.

In 2006 I married my Godly wife, Jackie, whom I thank God for, and in 2007 I became Chapter president of the local chapter of Full Gospel Businessmen in Massachusetts. God had given me Proverbs 8:4 when I asked Him if I should accept the leadership of this chapter. This is what it says : "To you , O men, I call out: I raise my voice to all mankind." I knew then that God called me to reach men in His name.

I do so and when I listen to Him, things seem to happen, when I get impatient and try to do things myself, we seem to go backwards. Thank God that He is faithful, even when I am not.

Blessings in Christ !!!

Don Rocci   Brockton, MA

Even as a child I obeyed my mother. I went to church weekly but I understood nothing. I was forced to go to Confession which horrified me because of going into that 'box' and speaking to somebody I could not see and also because I knew I was lying. I would make up things that would be and sound wrong even though I never thought about what my sins really were. I had no understanding of what was going on, so while church was going on I would have my own conversation with God.

As life progressed, although I received the sacraments, I came to the point of telling my mother that I got nothing out of it all even though I knew God was with me. I continued weekly going to church but it meant nothing. I knew that God was with me daily.

As a teen I did the regular teen things even though those things burdened me with guilt that would cause me to hibernate. Sin and hibernation became a cycle in my life. By the time I reached 19, I was at the point of being sick of my lifestyle but did not stop until I was 21 and met the man I later married.

It was New Year's Day of 1989. I was working and as I worked I was also praying, "Lord, I am so sick of all this. I'm done. Please either take me or make my life meaningful." That night I was out again with the girls. Only this night I met the man who would be my husband.

A few weeks after meeting him, he took me to meet his family at, of all places, church. I started going to church with him. Of course my parents did not know that as they would not approve, but it felt right inside of me and I felt I was being fed spiritual things and could finally understand and that made sense.

Then in August of 1990, my mother-in-law to be prayed with me to accept Jesus into my heart. That was just two months before we were to be married.

Now came tests. My Dad lost his job. Our invitations were ready to be sent, the hall, church, flowers, band – all were reserved. I had my gown and a wedding party of 27. The hall, band and invitations all were cancelled and then new ones found – with only 6 weeks left to the date.

Then we lost our wedding rings. My fiancé and I searched every box in the attic where we had put them. Through tears we were on our knees praying, thinking that God was forbidding our marriage when I suddenly got up and walked over to a box we had both been to several times looking and there they were – our rings. This was God's blessing and we both knew it. God was with us.

We were married and through life's regular trials my mother-in-law would pray with me and counsel me with scriptures. But because I could not yet understand I felt unworthy.

It was not until years later through many trials and tribulations when in 1997 I could finally, on my own, hear God speak to me. It was as if in 1990 when I asked Him in, He knew I was really not yet ready. So in His wisdom He waited 7 years until He knew it was perfect timing.

With the perfect timing came more attacks from Satan than I could ever have imagined. But now I had Christ in me and He got me through. Since then battles I would have walked away from before, I have stayed to fight.

That precious mother-in-law is gone. She is home with Jesus. My wonderful earthly father on whom I so depended is gone; he is with my Heavenly Father. Part of me feels abandoned but Christ in me keeps me going.

Today life is still a battle and my walk is rocky but Jesus is ever with me and keeps me going. All I want is to please Him until He calls me Home. I now know life will be a struggle and a battle but with Him in me I can prevail.

I want to add one more thing. In the middle of one of those battles God spoke ever so clearly telling me to do a thing most difficult and that ran totally against my grain. Yet I heard Him and I knew it. With His grace I was able to obey. I say this to encourage those who read this to obey Him as quickly as possible in whatever He may lead. Obedience is His way to blessing.

In 1989 when I prayed I thought my fiancé was His answer. In reality it was my mother-in-law God wanted me to meet in order to meet Him. His ways may seem strange but they are as He is – Faithful.

E.C. - Massachusetts

†

Both my parents were Christians before I was born so I was raised, happily, in a Christian family. I was "converted", as we would say back then, when I was nine years old. I was attending "Bible Adventure" (Good News Bible Club) at a local church one winter evening and I heard the gospel. Without the awareness or influence of my parents I immediately responded to the message. The two young ladies leading the Bible Adventure gave me a pocket New Testament, noting the occasion, which I still have.

Obviously, at age nine, I didn't have a full grasp of what I had decided. But as my life experiences and observations continued, and as I read and heard more, I never changed my mind. The seminal decision I made at that early age was the correct one!

My life was free of the really bad stuff, nonetheless I've had to fight some enemies of faith that are just as bad and maybe even more slick: passivity and doubt. During my college years I was immersed in an environment that rarely, if ever, acknowledged the existence of God, or "a god". Jesus Christ, of course, was never mentioned. Is there a better breeding ground for doubt and passivity?

I'm a career scientist, so I have some confidence in my own objectivity. This has allowed me to be wholly convinced that Jesus Christ is present in my life. As a scientist I understand chance and coincidence and with that understanding, I cannot attribute key events and occurrences in my life to anything except a real and present Jesus Christ.

Jim Yoder – Dauphin, PA

†

As I was growing up, my parents read the Bible to us daily, had Bible clubs in our home and taught us about who God is. They also took us to church every time the doors were open but "religion" wasn't about following a bunch of rules. It was about loving the God who loved us first. From an early age, I often heard about what Jesus had done for me on the cross, giving His life to take the punishment for MY sins. I knew that I had done wrong but didn't really want to admit it. In our Bible club they used to share every week about Jesus dying for our sins, coming to life again, and wanting us to come to Him for forgiveness. They gave us some cartoons in an envelope one week and, not being able to read yet at 5 years old, I wanted my Mom to read them to me. After a little story it would have the question, "Have you ever received Jesus as your Savior?" I didn't want her to read the question because I didn't want to have to answer it. I would always just answer, "I don't know." One week we went to a meeting similar to a Billy Graham Crusade. I don't remember anything he said except the statement, "If you don't KNOW that you are saved, then you probably aren't." I don't actually agree with that statement completely but God used it in my six year old heart. The next Thursday during Good News Club, when my mother gave the invitation to receive Christ, I raised my hand to show I wanted to. My Dad took me to my bedroom and helped me as I gave my life to Christ and received forgiveness of sin.

My life had many ups and downs spiritually over the years but God never let go of me and has continued to teach me more of Himself. I praise God for His continued work in my life.

Merrilea van den Akker - India

†

Joe's testimony - God's plan for my life.

God has blessed my wife, Khiengchai, and me with five wonderful children and a strong godly marriage for 15 years and counting. As I look back on my life I am so thankful for God's intervention in and willingness to use me as part of his greater plan - even though I never thought I had much to offer. I am also thankful for those who prayed for me and intervened with God on my behalf. While I'm sure I'll never fully understand the power of prayer, I know that it does free up the Holy Spirit to change lives.

Growing up, our family regularly attended church. Hard work and good morals were highly valued. With lots of siblings, there was lots of activity - not all of it particularly pleasing to God! To me, church for me was a place to see my cousins, play games in the gym, and explore around. We did love ringing the church bell after service and going through the line (multiple times) to shake the minister's hand. I think we were hoping that a few extra hand shakes would cover any potential "badness" in the week ahead!

I never really thought of myself as particularly bad even though I clearly knew I wasn't close to perfect. Once I hit junior high church attendance became more spotty - but I did attend the youth group at a Baptist church close to where we lived. God had already been at work changing the hearts of my older brothers as they started attending youth group and church. He had a lot of mercy on us. Some time along there (probably in answer to the prayers of my brothers) the Lord started pulling at my life as well. I wasn't ready to make a commitment but I also couldn't ignore His persistent call for me to surrender my life to Him.

Following my sophomore year in high school, I received a call from someone at the church asking if I would help with sports time at Vacation Bible School. I don't know why but I said yes I would. I ended up having a great time and the other guys helping out really welcomed me into their group of friends. They encouraged me to regularly attend the youth group and get involved in the fund activities. The funny thing was that everyone thought I was already a Christian - I knew the "language" well and could fake it - but I knew in my heart I hadn't really made Him Lord of my life. Later that fall at a youth group retreat, I knew it was time and I fully surrendered my life and asked Jesus to be my Lord and Savior. This marked the beginning of a very exciting adventure.

I went on to Wheaton College and continued my walk with the Lord. One particular chapel service touched me as I remember the President of the college explain how God could draw straight lines with crooked sticks. I didn't have to wait until I was perfect for Him to use me as part of His kingdom building! During that time God also led me into the Navigators ministry which was an integral part of deepening my faith and seeing the need to share our hope with non believers. I began to understand the importance of scripture memory and discipleship for young Christians to grow. The leaders were a very godly couple who had a true heart and strong passion for reaching the lost. Their impact on my life was incredible. To this day I remember many words of wisdom on how to handle life's challenges in a biblical way.

Upon graduating, I joined the Peace Corps and spent three years in West Africa. I had numerous opportunities to share my faith and live out what the Bible calls us to do. Many of the people where I lived asked questions about what I believed and we had great conversations about my faith. I also met a wonderful girl named Khiengchai who was also a volunteer in the same country. Several years later we married in Rochester, MN, and started our lives together.

My vision is to pass on our faith to our children and positively influence our neighborhood and community. I am so thankful for all the prayers of those who have known me. God's plan for me was much bigger than anything I could imagine and I am thankful for being a part of His Kingdom. I remind our children that each day we wake up that means that God has something for us to do to grow His Kingdom.

Joe Fulton - Minnesota

I was bought up in a religion but not a religious household. I was made to go to church when I was young even though my family did not go with me; but went on my own accord as I grew older because of the teaching I received in parochial school.

Within the confines of Catholicism I felt I knew the God I was taught. I felt wanted and loved and safe. I was not aware that Christianity was Protestant and Catholic. I did not know that until I was 26 years old, probably because I had no Protestant friends.

I was married and for five years did not attend church. Then I was divorced. After a year I met Paul. At that point I realized God was present in my life and was really there. Paul and I went to Pre-Cana conferences in the Methodist church and it was at that time I realized God was not just a Catholic.

We started a family – one, two, three, and raised them in the Methodist church. We did all the church stuff but something was missing and I knew it. I just did not know what was missing because I had a super ideal life. The super ideal moved to Norwell. The hole got bigger, the missing deeper.

We had a brush with Mormonism while still in the Methodist church. We were so progressive we were studying comparative religions. Today, looking back, I realize that was the Holy Spirit getting me ready.

A friend from Hull and Minister Marge went to a retreat and both found the Lord. They brought home a tape on how to be born again and how to be baptized in the Holy Spirit and gave it to me. I brought it home and listened to it on February 28, 1976. I knelt down and asked Jesus into my life. He came and He brought the Holy Spirit with Him. I got a 2-for-1 experience! To me it seemed a natural spiritual experience. I thought it was supposed to happen that way.

Life has never been the same. The walk began and now, 36 years later, through life's mountain top and valley experiences which include my having had cancer, the loss of my first-born adult child, the joys and sorrows with our children and life's regular marital challenges, I am here through the grace of God.

I have never ever been disappointed with the Lord's ways.

Janet Conboy – Norwell, MA

This last testimony is that of the man to whom this book is dedicated, my husband, Wim van den Akker. Written in 2008, he went Home to his Lord in 2009.

In the light of night flares we ran from our house to a backyard underground shelter. German aircraft were searching offensive targets to bomb and destroy. It was May 10, 1940. Germany invaded Holland. These, my earliest recollections, permanently impressed a 5-year old boy.

My father was an armament specialist in the Dutch Air Force, positioned in Soesterberg, the location of a military airfield to this day. He broke his leg during one of the air raids. To escape capture we moved quickly to different cities. Our final destination - the city of Groningen in the northern part of Holland, some 30 miles from the German border. It was located in the direct flight path that many allied bombers would fly in the last year of the war on their way to Germany.

Our family of one boy and three older girls was devoutly Catholic. My brother came later that year. Holland's strong religious divisions could be seen in church life as well as in entertainment and politics. German troops commandeered our parochial school and we children were forced to share the Protestant school buildings resulting in many physical and verbal fights between the traditionally divided camps.

Church attendance was very high. We attended Mass daily at the beginning of the school day. When old enough I served as an altar boy in a Catholic hospital that cared mostly for recuperating allied soldiers waiting to be shipped home.

Confidential confession to a priest was part of our regular church life. I was very disturbed when the priest told me he would speak to my parents if I continued to confess certain personal sins. It became a cornerstone in my attitude of mistrust of those in authority. I realized later that he probably had my best interest in mind.

I finished trade school at the age of 15 and started to work in a small electronics factory located between a big textile company and a legal house of prostitution. It became an introduction into a world that I had been shielded from till then.

Education was hard to come by and only reserved for a privileged few. I signed up for the army at the age of seventeen for six years, giving me the opportunity to go to electronics school for three years. Europe was being re-armed under NATO plan. Soldiers needed to be trained in all aspects of defense and war.

At the age of eighteen I was the youngest of five out of a class of 45 to be invited to attend a training with the United States Signal Corps in Fort Monmouth, New Jersey. This was an adventure that opened my mind to a different culture. This culture was not built around the framework of religion; it was built on the framework of its founders and a constitution that spoke about liberty and justice for all.

During this time I met some wonderful people, one of whom helped me settle in Kansas City, Missouri, when I immigrated in 1959. Throughout this time my religious beliefs came under constant questioning as I met people who had little or no religious convictions, or whose beliefs were quite different from my own.

The question of authority became paramount in my search for truth. I remember vividly a discussion about what constituted a mortal sin. The chaplain explained that anything willfully done against the known will of God was such a sin.

For a while I thought I might have a chance of deserving heaven, until I began to consider why should what he said be true? What infallible source of truth did he have? If the Pope was the only man infallible in spiritual matters, how could I be sure of any true religious answer seeing I would never speak to the Pope? Why could, or should, I believe those that represented him?

If I spoke to someone of a different faith, I would only get their answer on the same subject. Why should I believe them?

Around 1962, I concluded that all religious beliefs were strictly determined by culture, since most person's professional religion seemed to coincide with that of their parents. I failed to see what that had to do with truth. In many cases, only marriage into a different religion seemed to account for a change of religion. My question there also was, "What did that have to do with truth?"

I was reminded and impressed by a statement I read in a book called "Mansions of Philosophy" by W. Durant. The statement read, "It was as rare for a man to see truth as it was to see a falling star."

My last question, "Does God really exist?" scared me. I was quickly becoming a bystander, watching the parade and its spectators. I read about many religions in the Time Life Book of "The World's Great Religions." I did not embrace any of it. Going to a church of a different denomination did not solve my problem either; I wasn't ready for the message or they were not giving it.

In November 1963 I met a lovely Catholic girl named Barbara, my wife to be, just three weeks after arriving in Massachusetts from California. We were married on August 22, 1964 in St. Agatha's Church in Milton, Massachusetts. My continuing occupation with thoughts about God and religion had not stopped. Our first blind date had finished in a restaurant in Quincy talking about my most puzzling subject, God and religion. I was rapidly becoming an agnostic.

In the following ten years we had three children, two boys and one girl. The marriage that had started with a good measure of ideals had begun to unravel. I began to find peace in a bottle, but that wasn't peace at all, just a dulling of my senses.

My habits of smoking anything legal had been added to by drinking anything with alcohol in it.

The year 1974 was to be a different year. A co-worker by the name of Leon had become a good companion and friend. He was Catholic and a willing listener to my quest to understand religion and things pertaining to God. "Did I ever pray?" he asked. No, I didn't think that would help anything.

Actually I did pray occasionally when flying in turbulent weather and would make some promise to visit church on Saturday if I would just arrive safe at my destination.

Leon suggested I might like to attend a retreat. I was very open to that. More than once I had thought that if there was any reality to any of this you had to come into it as an adult. "You come to this retreat just the way you are," he said.

I did, with a case of beer, all my smoking supplies and two books, "The Theory of Evolution" by Darwin and Thomas Aquinas' "The Proofs of the Existence of God." I told Barbara if God existed something would happen. I didn't specify what.

The retreat started in a rather embarrassing way. You were asked to introduce yourself and what parish you came from. Though churched, Barbara and I rarely visited the local parish, and at any rate I didn't remember its name. I argued the relativity of religion for one day and had no converts. I discovered some people were praying for me, which I interpreted as an effort to manipulate.

The first evening, Thursday, I finished a six-pack by myself. By Friday evening I had stopped participating since any effort on my part to become a believer seemed to be going nowhere. They mentioned such things as the need to be born again and that faith was a gift from God.

When on Friday I was invited to participate in a written prayer, I wrote, "When I leave here I will continue to look for God." In the Friday evening chapel service my spiritual journey began to come to a head. I found myself crying for no apparent reason. It felt good but strange. I had not shed a tear for 15 years, except when in a melancholic mood because of excessive drinking.

My thoughts on what was happening varied from wanting to run out of the place and never visit a church again, to following it wherever it might lead. After all, I had said that if God existed, something would happen. I chose the latter and made a resolution on Saturday morning not to smoke just for that day. During the morning chapel service the invitation was again given to offer a personal prayer. Man had not given me any answer thus far. I didn't remember if I had ever asked God anything except in a somewhat superficial manner. I was at a crossroads, deciding to talk to God from my heart. Would I dare ask in front of all these men for the gift of faith? I don't remember the exact words, but I stood up and asked.

It wasn't until two hours later during a time in my retreat room my soul seemed set free from whatever had held it in bondage. I felt free, as if chains had been broken.

My mind was still not at rest, but something inside me said, "Wim, surrender yourself. I am here for you." I did respond to that invitation. Before the weekend ended, I had an opportunity to acknowledge my sins. I felt clean, a new man.

When asked to share about my closest moment with Christ, I quoted the Creed that I had so many times prayed as a young boy but which was never real until this day.

I bought a Bible that weekend and began to read and pray. "Lord, heal my marriage." God answered that prayer also.

No, not all our problems did go away, but we are still together after 43 years and I know beyond a shadow of a doubt that without God it would have ended a long time ago. I began to read the Bible that seemed a death book before. It had become and still is like bread from Heaven.

In the beginning I wondered, "Will I still believe it tomorrow?" Well, today is tomorrow 2008, 34 years later. I thank God daily for the gift He has given me. I have not always acted and lived the way I should in all these years. That is why Jesus came to bridge the gap between God and

Man. God is faithful. He is not like a man. I have come to know the truth.

Jesus Christ is the Son of God who died for my sins, was resurrected from the dead, and who will come again in Glory!!!

God has given me the gift I asked for and changed my life beyond anything I thought possible. During the retreat weekend my desire to smoke and drink disappeared without any withdrawal symptoms. I had many times before tried to stop smoking and drinking but never could.

God has abundantly blessed our life and those of our children. My wife and I together and individually have been involved in our church and a number of Christian layman organizations. As far as our professed church affiliation is concerned, we love Catholics as well as Protestants and people of all faiths. We meet at the foot of the Cross and ask the question.

Who do you think is that man? **Who has the answer?**

Jesus saith unto him, I am the way, the truth and life. No man cometh unto the Father but by Me. John 14:6

And this is the will of Him that sent Me, that every one which seeth the Son and believeth on Him may have everlasting life and I will raise him up at the last day. John 6:40

For God so loved the world that He gave His only begotten Son, that whosoever believes in Him should not perish but have everlasting life. John 3:16

†

TEN

My prayer is that by reading this book and these testimonies you have seen there are different places, as it were, for those who call themselves Christians. I have more or less centered in on three of those places, though there are certainly more.

One is for those who attend church and believe that because they do, or because they have said certain words, they are 'safe' where God and their forever life is concerned, whether or not they give God another thought during the week. Rather like the outer court in the Old Testament. They really are nowhere with God.

Another is for those who truly are born again but are afraid, for whatever reason, to have a deep and intimate relationship with God – Father, Son and Holy Spirit. This I equate to the inner court. They are there, but not quite as close as God would have them.

The place God desires for us is for those who have entered into the holy of holies. These are those who have a sweet, real and intimate, personal, breath by breath relationship with the Living God. These are those for whom Jesus is their very life.

God wants for all of us to be in that third group. That is the fellowship God meant for us to have in the atoning work of Jesus. Salvation is good and needful, for sure. But it is not enough to satisfy

l's desire for a love life with mankind – with
and with me. That veil was rent for a reason.
ants us to enter in.

He wants to be in every aspect of our lives.
Nothing is too small for His concern and notice. I
used to tell my Sunday school kids that God is like
your imaginary playmate except for one thing. God
is real. He is really there. His Word does not say,
"My sheep hear My voice." without reason. He
wants us to hear Him…to be in close union with
Him.

Once we come into the realm of the SO REAL our
job (and it is work) now is to stay there. Do not
settle for church on Sunday. Do not forego our own
study because we attend Bible study. Do not allow
ourselves to slowly slip back into complacency.

Church is good and so is Bible study, but if it is all
we have then we have fallen back into surreal
living. God wants us to be up close and personal
with Him, every day…and every minute of every
day. He wants us to study to show ourselves
approved unto Him. Dig into His Word and find
the nuggets of gold He has placed there for us and is
waiting to reveal them to us.

Jesus said it was expedient for us that He leave that
the Holy Spirit would come. It is His will that we
have a vital relationship with the Holy Spirit. No
need to fear Him. He will always lead us to Jesus.
He will always reveal truth from the Word. He will
never lead us astray.

Give Him tools to use. Go out and purchase a good concordance – Strong's or Young's. Get a good Bible dictionary. Have a King James along with your newer version when you study. The newer versions are okay for reading but study is enhanced by the richness of the depth of the King James language. It may feel different and therefore difficult at first, but it will grow on you and you will eventually enjoy its fullness.

When we show God we are serious about obeying His command to study His Word, He honors us by opening His Word up to us and showing us things that reveal more of who He is and how we are to live to be pleasing to Him. He shows us more and more the difference between the SURREAL and the SO REAL. His heart's cry is for us to remain in the SO REAL with Him.

We all want a pastor or a teacher to 'show us how' or to do it for us. But that is not possible in our life with God. When we stand before Him no one will join us. No pastor. No teacher. No friend. No mentor. No parent. No sibling. Only us and God. That's another reason why it is important for us to learn to live in that mode now. It may sound like a self-serving reason at first but we hopefully will come to the point where we live in such close union with God simply because He is worthy. Because it blesses Him. Because there really is nothing else, no one else deserving of all our being – our love, our time, our energy. All to God, that's REAL.

†

ELEVEN

Lately He's been showing me 'puzzle pieces'. Little bits of my life that I've listed on a piece of paper when He witnesses them to my spirit. At first I had no idea what it was all about other than that He had said 'puzzle pieces'. I have a list so far of about 20. I say 'about' because it is added to often. As I write them down I am beginning to get a glimpse of the picture, the truths, He is showing me with the puzzle pieces. I don't have the whole picture yet, but I do know it has to do with the plan God has for my life.

Ephesians 2:10 tells us that God has a plan for each of our lives. He ordained that plan before we were ever born. It is there, waiting for us to fulfill it.

So often we want what we do not have and probably will never have. We think, "Oh, if only…." But if only's are not real. They are a form of our rebellion against what is real and can, if we are not careful, slowly draw us away from that real relationship and God's plan for us and we can drift away before we even know what has happened.

Do not misunderstand. I do not mean to say that we should not try to educate ourselves and always be learning new things. Not at all. We should, in fact. But to not be satisfied with our lot in life is a totally different matter.

There are some (lots of) things in our lives that we cannot change. Things that God arranged. Things that God ordained. For example: where we are born, the parents to whom we are born, our siblings, our DNA (this is really big because it is who we are individually and in every way). These are the things by which He grows us up and teaches us spiritual truths – His REAL. I believe these are our puzzle pieces along with other things He brings into our lives and we need to learn to cooperate with His grace and mercy and wisdom and allow them to mature us as He would wish.

This is when we need to stay really close to Him because some of these things are not pleasant and we will be tempted to be drawn away from them both by our own flesh and peer pressure.

Remember, God tells us that He does not want our sacrifices. He wants us to know Him. Only when we are in such a close personal relationship with Him will we be at the point where we will dig our heels in and obey when He speaks. Only then will we overcome our fear of man (being thought a bit nuts by others, being rejected by peers, etc.) and fear God more than man. That's God's REAL.

Substituting this for doing all the religiously correct outward things is easier and feels better, but it is totally SURREAL where God is concerned. Unless we are willing to draw near to God – the resurrected Lord Jesus Christ – and let Him draw near to us, we are living our religious life in the SURREAL.

Many years ago there was a poster with Uncle Sam pointing his finger at you and it read "Uncle Sam wants you." Well, God wants you. That's the reason Jesus came. God wants us. He wants us in spirit and in truth. He wants us to seek for Him with all our heart and mind and strength. That's work for sure, but well worth the effort. If one wants the gold one has to dig for it. Hard work. There is no greater treasure than finding the Living God, or better spoken, being found of Him. Our whole eternity depends upon it.

†

TWELVE

Let me give you another example of SURREAL
today in Christian circles. While I agree that what
comes out of our mouth is important, I do not agree
with the current teaching that if we are ill and we
say we are well that we will become well.

That is simply not living in reality. Rather to say
that I'm not well but I'm going to do what I can and
then give it to God and ignore it. That may sound
and even be a bit foolish but at least it is REAL.

Jesus is the Truth. If we want to walk with Him we
must walk in the Truth. Simple as that.

For example. I have arthritis. It is becoming
progressively worse. The meds don't want to work
anymore. Part of arthritis is depression. I don't
know how that figures in, but it does. Everything
I've read lists it as a component in arthritis. I can
attest to its being true.

Now for me to say I don't fight depression every
day would not be true. I do fight it. If I don't I fall
into it; so, I'm not depressed but only because I
fight it.

If I have a cold, I'm not going to say I don't have a
cold. I'm going to take what I need to fight the
cold. And keep on praising God while I cough and
sneeze, until He either heals me or the cold runs its
course.

I say all this because teaching today says we should never make a 'negative' confession. Well, truth is sometimes negative. Jesus was depressed! (Matt. 26:38 and Mark 14:34) David was depressed! Read the Psalms. It is all there. We do not live in depression, we fight it. But to say we do not have it is not truth.

To say "I'm not going to accept that." – whatever 'that' might be when 'that' is as plain as the nose on one's face is ludicrous. It does not help us win people to Jesus nor does it please Jesus. Truth sets people free. Truth makes people REAL. That is step one.

How we handle the truth after we've accepted it will determine if we become bitter or better.

It is one thing to accept the truth it is another to accept it from God's loving hand as His plan for our lives. That is step two.

If we do not like what He has brought to us and we become angry and rebellious, we will be bitter, angry, frustrated and unforgiving. If we agree with Him and allow Him to have His way in our lives – in our minds and hearts – we will be pleasing to Him, have peace in our minds and joy in our hearts – even in the midst of pain be it physical or emotional.

Remember, if we look at what He has done or is doing in another's life and try to mimic it or make law out of it we are slipping once again into SURREAL. The only REAL with God is one on one with Him. God and you. God and me. God wants us to be together with each other in worship and fellowship, but not when it interferes with our own personal relationship with Him. God is first. All others secondary. That's His REAL.

†

THIRTEEN

I have repeated myself often in this book. That was
on purpose.

Hopefully when we hear it or read it enough, we
will believe that God loves us and wants to be close
to us. He wants to be in all our thoughts. He does
not want to be important in our life. He wants to
BE our life. He must be the reason we take our next
breath. He wants to guide and lead and direct our
lives. He wants to be our strength and the reason
we get out of bed each morning.

This is not because of God's ego. It is because He
chooses to bless us and prove Himself to us so that
we can see and experience first hand that it is not
we ourselves but Him working in us that
accomplishes all that we do and have become. He
wants to show us how big He is and how able He is
in order that we might trust Him more and praise
Him for where He has us and how we might serve
Him.

No one can do this for us. It must be one-on-one
with God. No pastor or teacher can give this to us.
If this is what we want we must go to God alone
and allow Him to work His work in our lives as
only He is able. That's REAL.

†

FOURTEEN

Before I was a Christian had someone held a gun to my head and told me to renounce Jesus or they'd pull the trigger I'd have told them to shoot. So steeped was I in religion.

But when God revealed Jesus to me He took me out of the darkness and brought me into His marvelous Light. That is how I knew I had been in darkness.

Another thing He did was to wipe the 'cobwebs' from my mind. He showed me that as a child I perceived things I could not handle and therefore shut off my ability to reason. When I think back I wonder I ever made it to age 33 which was where I was when He revealed Himself to me.

In school I had to memorize everything to get the grades I did but I understood nothing. It amazes me that it was not until high school that anyone picked up on that. It was my Problems of Democracy teacher who told me I could not see the forest for the trees. She was right. It sounds humorous now but I had no idea what she was talking about back then.

But when Jesus came in He showed me that He was cleaning those self-inflicted cobwebs out of my place of thinking. Now it was empty and I devoured the Word for hours every day to fill it up.

However, each time I would get to the book of Job the old confusion would descend upon me again.

So I told the Lord that I was not going to read that book and since He knew where I lived, when He was ready to reveal its meaning to me I'd be home.

He did! One morning as I came down to be with Him before my family arose I was in the New Testament when once again my head became a funnel and knowledge of the book of Job was poured in.

I sat there amazed. I said to Him, "I wasn't even in the Old Testament!" Then I said to myself that I had to go to Job and test out what I had just received to be sure it was from God.

It was! There in the book of Job, in part, was my testimony.

The clue to the book (as we mentioned in section FIVE) is found in its last chapter in verses 5 and 6. There we find the result of a man who met God and went from SURREAL to SO REAL! Job makes the classical statement:

"I have heard of Thee by the hearing of the ear: but now mine eye seeth Thee. Wherefore I abhor myself, and repent in dust and ashes."

Job was taken from being deeply religious and brought into a living relationship with the Living God! The reason the confusion came back on me when reading it was because I was not looking at the book of Job for what it was.

Job had heard of God…but seeing Him brought Job into a totally different sphere.   Job went from SURREAL to SO REAL.

†

FIFTEEN

If you have read this book I am praying for you.
My prayer, coupled with God's promises in His
Word, assures you of grace sufficient enough for
you to have all you need to turn to God and humble
yourself before Him, asking for His salvation by the
blood of the Lamb of God, the Lord Jesus Christ.

Allow Him to reveal Himself to you. Allow Him to
gift you with what no other being can give to you,
that gift being Himself, of course.

Jesus promised in John 5:24 "Verily, verily, I say
unto you, He that heareth My Word and believeth
on Him that sent Me hath everlasting life and shall
not come into condemnation; but is passed from
death into life." When Adam ate of the fruit in the
Garden of Eden he suffered spiritual death. God
now offers us something far better than Adam ever
knew. Adam had stipulations – do not eat.... In
Christ Jesus we have the promise of eternal life,
born again of incorruptible seed.

We can be sure of Heaven. We can live without the
weight of the world on our shoulders. We can have
hope no matter what life on this earth brings our
way. Better – we can rest in the knowledge that we
will be with Him, the Lord Jesus Christ, forever and
ever. We do not have to work for it, we cannot earn
it. All we need do is go to God and receive it from
His all too willing hand. John 6:37b is a promise
Jesus made to all men of all time, "...and him that

cometh to Me I will in no wise cast out." So come. It is God's will that all be saved. "For this is good and acceptable in the sight of God our Savior; Who will have all men to be saved and to come unto the knowledge of the truth. For there is one God and one mediator between God and men, the man Christ Jesus." – 1 Timothy 2:3-5

The only thing keeping us from Him and all He has for us is ourselves. God loves you. It is true, it is an amazing story, this life of Christ Jesus. But God's methods are not ours and His ways and thoughts far above anything we can even begin to comprehend. If we could understand it all, we'd be God.

We have nothing to lose by humbling ourselves before Him and in total honesty of heart and mind bow before His majesty and accept His way. This I can promise, you will not be sorry.

One final word: Always remember, this is not about religion – it is about Jesus. First last and always, it is about Jesus.

Other books by Barbara van den Akker:

A New! Weapons That Make You Win

ABC's of Walking with God - organized with an index that's alphabetized to guide the reader to a point of reference that includes scripture referrals and personal experience on emotions, eating, thinking, marriage, forgiveness, self-control and much more.

Two Minute Thoughts on Living with the Living God - an extremely creative 70 page devotional that gives direction and answers to so many questions...

Mariah & Miranda Series - four books in one it is the story of two little girls who travel back and forth from the natural realm to the land of imagination where amazing things happen to them to help develop moral concepts upon which to live their lives as rulers of their father's kingdom. For those who have eyes to see there is much spiritual truth here! A great bedtime story for the young and the young at heart...

All books available on Amazon and Kindle

For more information:

Barbara van den Akker
1554 Ocean Street
Bldg #7 Unit #224
Marshfield, MA 02050
781-837-0026
bvdakker@thayerscale.com

38917598R00085

Made in the USA
Middletown, DE
17 March 2019